ARDSLEY'S

DYNASTY

1986-1989

When the Village's High School Ruled New York State Baseball

Bruce Fabricant

ARDSLEY'S DYNASTY – 1986-1989
When the Village's High School Ruled New York State Baseball

ISBN-13: 978-1720347187

ISBN-10: 1720347182

For all information, contact:
Bruce Fabricant
E-Mail: bfabric459@aol.com

To Robin and Vicki
and to Neil Fitzpatrick and his Ardsley boys who played
on a high school field
that now exists only in memory

ALSO BY BRUCE FABRICANT

That Perfect Spring

Baseball Boys
Rediscovering 1950s Little League Baseball in Mount Vernon, NY

Remembering Mount Vernon, NY
The Place We Called Home

Mount Vernon, NY Sports Champions Heroes & Legends

ACKNOWLEDGMENTS

On a sunny Saturday in April 2017 I received a package in the mail from Neil Fitzpatrick. It was a lengthy memoir about his youth and coaching career. It came with a note suggesting that I use it as I saw fit which I did. So I am deeply indebted to Neil for his heartfelt essays about all things baseball and about life. I also thank him for the two lengthy interviews we had in Greenburgh and in Somers about his Ardsley baseball boys and their march to history.

Then there are Coach Fitz's players, now in middle age with families of their own, who shared their thoughts about growing up in Ardsley, playing on championship teams, and bonding with friends for a lifetime. Special thanks goes to Jeff Caldara who Coach Fitz called his greatest captain. Jeff is still the leader. When he first heard about this project he was on board immediately. He put me in touch with players from all four championship teams, each of whom gladly, enthusiastically and warmly told me about their Ardsley experiences: the 1986 team, Billy Bakker, C.J. Russo, and George Phillips; 1987, Brian Lepore and Ray DiMartino; 1988, Mike Ferraguzzi and Jeff Caldara; 1989, Tom Caldara and Tom Ferraguzzi; and 1982, Greg Fonde.

I also wish to thank Peter Marcus of the Ardsley Historical Society and Historian Richard Borkow. I am deeply indebted to all of you. Lastly, a thank you to my favorite Ardsley Panthers, Robin Fabricant Pagano and Vicki Fabricant Jeffery.

TABLE OF CONTENTS

INTRODUCTION

In mid-August of 1781 General George Washington hoisted his 6 foot 2 inch frame onto his horse and left his headquarters located in the Joseph Appleby farm house along the present day Secor Road in Ardsley, New York.

He was on his way to review much of his American Continental army that was camped on the north side of Heatherdell Road, in the area of today's Ardsley High School.

There on August 14 the general received one of the most momentous messages of the entire Revolutionary War. If he and French general Comte de Rochambeau could quickly move the Continental and French armies from New York to Virginia it might be possible to trap England's General Cornwallis' troops gain a decisive victory and end the war.

Two months later the victory of the allied American and French forces at Yorktown led to uncontested independence for the United States.

Fast forward more than two hundred years. Another general of sorts achieved fame that is everlasting in Ardsley's and New York's sports history. This general did it on the same high school soil that Washington knew so well. Neil Fitzpatrick is that little general, six inches shorter than Washington. Fitzpatrick didn't lead men into war. He did however lead Ardsley High School's varsity baseball team to heights no other New York state high school team has ever reached.

For four successive years, 1986 through 1989, Ardsley captured the Class C New York State Public High School Athletic Association baseball championship. Each year the Ardsley Panthers beat out more than 125 high schools. That was never accomplished before and hasn't been done since. Winning the New York State championship two years in a row is the closest any school has come.

For the hundreds of Ardsley faithful who annually made the trek upstate New York to watch their teams play in championship games, there was nothing like the site of the boys spilling from a dugout and meeting on the diamond in joyous celebration. All who were there knew something great had happened that would never be forgotten.

Now you might glaze over these numbers. So take a moment and read them twice. Let Neil's success but more importantly Ardsley's success sink in.

In Fitzpatrick's 17 years as a varsity coach his teams won four state championships, five regional titles, six sectional championships and 10 league titles. Coach Fitz won a total of 306 games and lost 111 for a 74 percent winning percentage.

How good is that? The great New York Yankees manager Casey Stengel won five straight World Series from 1949 through 1953. Over those five seasons he had a 63 percent regular season winning percentage. That's eleven percentage points lower than Fitzpatrick's total career numbers.

There's more. During his coaching career, Neil averaged 18 wins and 6 losses per year. His 30-year tenure at Ardsley included coaching baseball (Freshman, JV, and Varsity) and even a little basketball. He also started and coached the soccer program during the 1970s.

These are just the numbers. He did so much more. He brought an entire Ardsley community together, inspired folks from Ashford Avenue to Heatherdell Road to Wood Avenue with championships. He taught youngsters how to master fundamental baseball skills that turned dreams into reality. He taught the game as well as anyone ever has in Westchester County. Most importantly, he helped his players become better persons.

A key ingredient to Fitzpatrick's success was his simple credo, ignore the past and just focus on the present. That's hard to do. Keeping a one game at a time attitude epitomized all his championship teams. They didn't think about past victories or worry about living up to their reputations.

Jeff Caldara knows Neil Fitzpatrick better than any of the coach's former players. Caldara was a key player, the shortstop on Coach Fitz's 1987 and 1988 teams. He's coached Ardsley's baseball varsity since 1998 when he succeeded Fitzpatrick.

"Coach was a man who you earned your respect from," Caldara said. "He treated us all like adults. He never over-coached and, as long as you did the right thing, he didn't bother you. He left you alone and gave us a freedom that you never thought you could have in sports. He was a huge influence on me and how I try to coach."

Coach of the year is an interesting award in Westchester County New York. "I earned it many times but I remember telling my teams that the players should vote for it but only after they reach adulthood and have kids and jobs of their own," Fitzpatrick said. "Because a great coach, at least for high school kids, is one who has players who can look back and say, 'that man helped me be a better person.' Right now, I'm thinking of all the guys I coached and wondering if they have fond thoughts of me.

"I think a lot of my success with my baseball teams was that I was rooting for my players to feel the thrill of success but certainly not demanding it. As proud as I was of my practice sessions, I always felt what I brought to my teams had more to do with an attitude. A big part of that attitude was never to embarrass a player in public."

There are many theories as to what made Neil Fitzpatrick such a good baseball coach. Maybe it was his strategy. For sure it was his ability to get the most out of his players, many of whom who you will meet in these pages like C.J. Russo, Billy Bakker, George Phillips, Brian Lepore, Steve Gyimesi, Ray DiMartino, Mike and Tom Ferraguzzi, Tom and Jeff Caldara, Bernie McNerney, and many more. And yet, perhaps Coach Fitz's biggest contribution was his knowledge of baseball fundamentals and his insistence that his players know them.

His practices were two hours long. That's it, two hours, and no longer. Every minute was planned. His players would go over every game situation. By the time the games came along his boys didn't have to think. They just had to react because of what he instilled in them.

Times change and people move on. Memories of that magical four year run fade. Plenty of people don't know anything about Coach Fitz and the youngsters who made New York State baseball history.

Early on, a sign saluting the '86 and '87 champions was in front of the high school where the current baseball field is. That sign disappeared. New signs were erected like one at the corner of 9A and Ashford Avenue, across the street from where the annual Christmas tree once stood. That also is gone. All that remains at Ardsley High School is the trophy case with a section devoted to baseball. Sectional, regional and state plaques are there along team pictures.

But what does remain are fading memories and newspapers that forever capture statistics and game stories. I looked through numerous scrapbooks that documented Ardsley's diamond exploits that were recorded in newspapers like *The White Plains Reporter Dispatch,* to be remembered for all time, just as they happened. I visited that city's library four times. Now, many of Ardsley's games are summarized here with a section devoted to each championship season.

I also found a group of men who played on those title teams who were eager to talk about the village they grew up in and their journeys to high school championships. I also spent hours sitting and talking to Neil Fitzpatrick. This book is a testament to him and what he accomplished. It's also recognition to the Ardsley teenagers who made New York State sports history. So come back with me and relive those glory days of Ardsley baseball.

Bruce Fabricant, 2018
bfabric459@aol.com

SUMMER BASEBALL

1. MAKING A DIFFERENCE

What made Ardsley High School 80's baseball era so great?

Through the years Coach Fitzpatrick was asked that question countless times. He had an unwavering answer. It was simply summer baseball for youngsters and teenage boys.

That makes total sense. Ardsley's Little League baseball gave the boys a strong foundation on which to build. In time, for many of these youngsters success followed them to high school.

If you were a kid playing Ardsley Little League baseball in the seventies and eighties you had your big shrines like Yankee Stadium and Shea Stadium. For generations, these ballparks were where fathers and sons bonded.

But these same youngsters had their own Ardsley diamonds at McDowell Park and Macy Park. They were ball fields that were simple, basic, with no frills attached.

McDowell Park located on Heatherdell Road near the Sprain Parkway was named after B. William McDowell, who served as Ardsley Police and Village Justice for 41 years and as Greenburgh Town Justice of the Peace for 16 years. McDowell Park, dedicated in 1956, wasn't the only place to play. Teams practiced sometimes at Macy Park and also at Secor Woods Park, just off of Secor Road.

There weren't many better places to spend summer days learning the game. Even today, most who played in that era remember running out onto the diamond feeling giddy when the game was about to begin. They remember smacking the pocket of their first baseball glove and chanting the name of their starting pitcher while crouching in the infield waiting for a grounder.

"If you want to talk Ardsley baseball, you have to go back to the Little League fields," said Tom Ferraguzzi, who caught on Ardsley's championship '89 squad. "The big guys took control."

C.J. Russo, a three year starter in '85, '86, and '87 couldn't agree more.

"It's parents, a community, it's Little League. We had really good quality coaches in Little League who taught us the fundamentals of the game. They were hard on us. We practiced hard. We played hard. It just kind of progressed and JV was just a portion of the progress. And then we got to Fitz. It was a whole other level but we were prepared to work and play hard."

Fitzpatrick often talked about Ardsley's unique environment. "We had great kids from great families who all rooted, not only for their own kids, but for the team to be successful. And, we had a great Little League and Babe Ruth program in place.

"High school baseball is the icing on the cake. The substance of a ball player's career takes place in the hot and humid double headers of July and August. To be a successful high school baseball player, you need to keep playing over the summer, and Ardsley gave them the opportunity. They also got some great coaching."

Guiding, teaching, and encouraging Ardsley's pre-teen and teenage boys early on were a group of men who lovingly provided countless hours of instruction. Some of these men knew the fundamentals better than others. But they all had the interest of the kids at heart.

The essence of that Ardsley Little League experience was what happened between each youngster and his coach. The coaches taught not only how to play the game, they soothed egos, and built self-confidence.

Among the men who laid the groundwork for Ardsley's future success were Dennis Corelli, Charley Russo, Steve Murphy, Fred Calaicone, Joe Presbyto, Dan Minozzi, Fred Arone, Roy Stephens, Frank Jazzo, Roy Stephens, Lou Ferraguzzi, Gene O'Gull, Carmine Pagano, and Don McNerney.

There was one man however mentioned more often than anyone

else, Mike DiMartino, who began his coaching career teaching fundamentals to his three sons, Ray, Mike and Ed, who all later played for Coach Fitz.

"I remember watching Mike talk to his summer teams," Fitzpatrick said. "He was pretty adamant about discipline. You could tell it from his boys who were a pleasure to coach.

"In a way he made my job easier. My players thought I wasn't a shock for them to play for in a disciplined way because they had that from Mr. DiMartino."

Mike Ferraguzzi from the '87 and '88 teams remembered how he was afraid to make a mental mistake when he played for DiMartino.

"If you made a physical mistake playing for Mr. DiMartino, or Brian Connolly our JV coach or later Coach Fitz, there was no problem. Mental mistakes were inexcusable. It all started with Mr. DiMartino. He was extremely knowledgeable, extremely fair."

Mike Ferraguzzi's younger brother Tommy who caught for the high school in '89 and '90 said that Ardsley baseball needed Mike DiMartino. "He was the man who instilled discipline in all of us at an early age. When he coached in the Babe Ruth League I was scared to death of him. He wasn't mean. He was firm. He was personal friends with my parents. I would say to my dad, how can you even go out with him?

"The Babe Ruth years, 13-14-15, that was when we realized when we stepped on the field it was a different type of discipline. Mike DiMartino was the catalyst who provided the discipline and how you held yourself on the field."

DiMartino provided some funny moments as well. George Phillips who starred on Coach Fitz's first state championship team in '86 said, "I was a big kid and could hit balls over the fence. Mike DiMartino was throwing batting practice to me and I hit one deep to left center. Mike says, 'Oh, that's a good shot son'.

Mike threw another pitch and George hit it out again. This time Mike said, "You made me do it. I have to do it. You hit one off me, ok. You hit two and you're going down." George laughed and recalled how Mike threw it right at his head.

Greg Fonde graduated from Ardsley in 1983 and missed the

championship runs. He remembered the early days when he played Little League and later caught for two Fitzpatrick teams.

"Greg and his *Dugout News* is one of my favorite memories of all time," Fitzpatrick said.

Fonde joyfully made light of events happening in the high school. He did it over the school's intercom and in printed pages that were placed on the bulletin board outside the cafeteria. Fonde was a precursor of Robin Williams in the *Good Morning Vietnam* movie.

"Greg was a great student, not just a ball player," Fitzpatrick said. "He was a serious student and he must have spent a lot of time every night typing out *Dewey's Dugout News*. It was fantastic.

"Once we won a string of early season games. We were April and O. Not like 6-0 but April and O. On the last day of April Greg writes in his *Dugout News*, "Hold the May O."

"Fonde contributed some other wonderful lines. We had a great basketball fan section when Fonde was in high school. It was called the Cat House because it was a crazy rooting section. Then the wrestlers started calling their little gym the Mat House. When it was spring time and baseball, Fonde came up with the phrase, That's our Bat House.

"I started playing ball in 1970," Fonde recalled. "There was no soccer, no football, no basketball except for recreational Saturdays. So baseball was a big deal.

"A parade started off the season. It went through town down to McDowell Park and its three baseball diamonds. The signature field was for 11 and 12-year-olds. If you were good enough, you thought you could go to Cooperstown and the Hall of Fame.

"McDowell Park also served a great hamburger. It came from Louie's supermarket. At McDowell Park that there were usually 12 games a year. During the games, your team had to donate its time, maybe one or two games a year to work in the snack bar. They had ice cream, hot dogs, candy bars and soda but no granola bars. There was no such thing as bottled water.

"We had a dozen balls that we used in practice. They were water logged and dirty. We had maybe one metal bat that had dings in it. This was Ardsley during the early days of Little League baseball."

NEIL FITZPATRICK

2. NEIL OF COLLEGE POINT

As the Vietnam War raged in 1971, Neil Fitzpatrick faced a crossroads. He could either serve in the military or do something else.

The something else was to become a teacher. While he didn't know it at the time, Fitzpatrick had the makings of becoming a good teacher and even a better coach. Coaching was what he wanted to do with his life.

"While others went into the Peace Corps, I thought I could make teaching in high school a service to the country," Fitzpatrick said. "I never wanted to coach in college or at any other level other than high school. Maybe that's why God let me have so many championships. He knew my heart was in the right place."

Fitzpatrick looked at his teaching and coaching career differently than others might have looked at theirs.

"A lot of teachers can't wait to get out of the classroom and into administration. Many high school coaches look at the job as a mere stepping stone leading to a prestigious career. I had the satisfaction of being a New York state championship coach. But that wasn't why I became a coach."

"All the league, sectional and state championships were icing on the cake for me. Like actor Burt Lancaster said in the movie *Jim Thorpe – All American,* I just wanted to be called coach."

While Fitzpatrick found it a thrill every time his team won a league title, he especially looked forward to the halfway mark each season and hoped that he had accumulated enough wins to ensure a .500 season.

He never forgot the impact his former coaches had on his life especially his high school basketball and baseball coach Hugh Kirwan.

And even today Neil remembers the phrase, 'the ball played havoc with the right field wall'. It was from a local newspaper article that someone had cut out from a scrapbook. The story was about a Knights of Columbus softball game when Neil's dad Connie Fitzpatrick hit the shot. Neil was only twelve at the time.

"I had many baseball memories before that but this one was really important," he said. "My father had just died when I came across the article and said to my mom, 'Look mom, he played second base just like me.' I'm not even sure my father was a very good athlete but at the age of twelve I knew that baseball was in my blood."

That incident allowed Neil to open a line of communication with his mourning mom, Margaret, who at the age of 45 was just beginning her journey as a single mother to Jim, who was 18, Gerry 14, Neil 12, Lois 11, Ellen 5, and Brian 1.

By that age Neil was good enough to play baseball in older brother Jim's sandlot games.

"One of the clichés I always felt was true was 'from the cradle' which meant to be a good ballplayer you have to start young," he said.

Neil Fitzpatrick was born March 28, 1948 and lived in College Point, a working middle-class neighborhood in the New York City borough of Queens, located north of Flushing on Flushing Bay and the East River. The words "hidden" and "tucked away" are spoken when locals are asked to describe College Point.

Home to Neil was a white stucco house at 23-42 125th Street that his father bought for five thousand dollars. The doors were always open and the egg delivery man would walk in when the family was sleeping. Neil shared a bedroom with his two brothers while his three sisters shared another room.

Fitzpatrick said that his start in sports and baseball cannot overdo the magic provided by his mother. "She would trick me into having two pieces of celery placed around a carrot. She told me it was a hot dog."

Neil started pursing his passion to play baseball with his mother driving him and his American Legion teammates to games. Family chores or obligations never got in the way of a game.

His brother Jim found a job for him as busboy and valet at Cresthaven Country Club in Whitestone, New York. Never mind how many hours he was logging at the club, he would always get a ride to the next game.

"People thought I had a chance to make it but it was too big a leap for me," Fitzpatrick said. Neil was thirteen when a team that didn't have enough players let him suit up for a game. That might have been the first time he played on 90-foot base paths.

College Point also gave Neil his first hero, Junie Meyers, who was a shortstop and played for the Point in the highly competitive Queens Alliance League that featured former major leaguers and others looking to make baseball a career.

Neil never forgot Junie, a New York City garbage man whose route included Neil's block. It was all because of Junie's friendliness.

"Junie was probably aching like crazy from all the lifting but he always had a big smile and a 'Hi Nemo' when I saw him. "That's what they called me. I wanted to be as classy as Junie Meyers."

Herb Carroll was Neil's first real baseball coach. "He instilled a great deal of confidence in me," Fitzpatrick said. "Any time he talked to other coaches, he would tell them that I was destined to make it to the big leagues.

"I was 5 foot 6 inches tall when I was a freshman at Mater Christi High School and weighed less than 100 pounds. But Coach Carroll loved my spirit and bragged about me to whoever would listen. His expression that I took to heart was 'don't blow your own horn.'"

At Mater Christi Neil played both basketball and baseball. There Neil's future coaching career was shaped by his high school basketball and baseball coach Hugh Kirwan.

"He was not only a great athlete but he also carried himself so elegantly and that's why I modeled my coaching after him," Neil said. "He never screamed to get attention. His huddles were always calming and had a sense of purpose.

"Like Kirwan, I didn't reprimand a player in front of other people.

Coaching during a game should be between you and the player. All too often, a coach yells out to a player, 'You're supposed to hit the cutoff man for the throw to third' loud enough so that spectators know that it wasn't the coach's fault. The coach might even add, 'Didn't we just do that in practice yesterday?'

"What I would discipline myself to do when those mistakes happened was talk to the player between innings when spectators wouldn't know about it."

After graduating high school, Fitzpatrick entered Manhattan College where he played second base and later shortstop for the Jaspers. In his third year of varsity ball, Neil was selected All New York City Metropolitan Honorable Mention. He graduated with a B.S. degree in physical education and then a Masters in Health Education from the University of Maryland.

With a degree in hand, it was time for Neil Fitzpatrick to get a job. That's when his Manhattan baseball coach told him about two teaching jobs. One was on Long Island and the other in a village called Ardsley in Westchester County New York.

3. FIRST TIME IN ARDSLEY

In 1971Neil Fitzpatrick got the telephone call. He had an interview at Ardsley High School for a job teaching health. He barely knew where Ardsley was.

Neil to this day believes Ardsley's athletic director Tom Lindgren, who also was a Manhattan College alumni like himself, put in the final word that got him the job.

Dressed in his suit and wearing a tie, Fitzpatrick drove his brand new 1971 yellow Toyota Corolla north to Westchester County for that interview. It was a little more than 19 miles from College Point to Ardsley, about a 30 minute car ride. He drove up the Sprain Parkway and got off at Jackson Avenue and headed to the school.

Neil was in the country and Ardsley was an unknown destination. He would soon find out that Ardsley was just seven miles north of the Bronx. Ardsley's hilly, forested terrain made it seem much further away to Neil. It didn't take long for him to find himself on Ashford Avenue, a main road between two ridges that Indians once walked along from the Hudson River to the Long Island Sound. Years later, George Washington used that same road on his way to Yorktown.

There were places near Ardsley Square that would in time capture Neil's attention. Places like Riccio's Delicatessen, Captain Video, Ardsley Kosher, Liggett Rexall, Sinapi Pizzeria, Sunny Texaco and Marty's Mug & Munch were all popular destinations.

Neil's arrival in 1971 wasn't the major educational news in Ardsley that year. The town's new Ardsley Middle School was welcoming grades 5 through 8 for the first time.

Thirteen years earlier in 1958, after a long search for an additional school site for Ardsley's burgeoning school district, another building was completed at the top of what had formerly been the 356-acre Adolph Lewisohn estate. It initially housed grades 7 through 12. But after 1971, the same year Fitzpatrick began teaching, the school was only for traditional high school grades.

Fitzpatrick's first year in Ardsley was an eye opener for the young teacher. He admitted he was befuddled teaching health. "It was a disaster," he said. "I was not very good. I was struggling so much that I was ready to leave the teaching profession.

"I remember going home to College Point and getting called out by my mother. She said, 'Are you going to quit?' He didn't quit. Instead, Neil hung in and received much needed support from both Larry Dwyer, the school's guidance counselor, and from Tom Lindgren.

Lindgren also saw something in Fitzpatrick that he liked. He asked Neil to start a soccer program.

"I explained to him that I never played the game," Fitzpatrick said. "But Lindgren, being a physical education graduate of Manhattan College like me, said, 'You were prepared at Manhattan to coach all sports.'" Neil fumbled around learning the game but soon grew to love it. He also helped coach track that first year.

But baseball was the sport Neil loved. That's what he really wanted. When he arrived in '71, Bill Graney was the varsity coach and Hank Tina handled the junior varsity.

Neil wasn't shy. That first spring he went to one of Graney's practices and hustled out to second base and began taking ground balls with the kids, particularly with the second baseman Frank Cilurzo. Graney saw that Neil loved the game and soon asked him to start a freshman baseball team. That was his first job coaching baseball at Ardsley.

Every day his team took a bus to practice at Macy Park on Saw Mill River Road since the varsity was using the field behind the high school. And for the next 10 years Fitzpatrick was on the diamond coaching fledgling freshman and junior varsity ballplayers and loving every minute of it.

"I was lucky that Bill Graney was about to retire when I was just about ready to move up from freshman to varsity," Fitzpatrick said. "I never consulted with the junior varsity coach Hank Tina. In retrospect, that was a bit pushy on my part but Hank handled it with class and I went on to coach two of his boys, John and Michael, Hank Tina and I are good friends to this day."

Neil Fitzpatrick was now Ardsley's varsity baseball coach. He knew plenty about the game. He quickly learned about the late winter and early spring weather in Ardsley and how it would play havoc with his practices. Drizzle and snow moved many a March practice indoors. The players got by with sock balls and tennis balls.

Those indoor practices were something his players never forgot. Fitzpatrick remembers shopping in New Jersey on Route 17 and wondering how he could find a baseball that he could use in the gym. The balls would be rolled up socks.

C.J. Russo, one of Coach Fitz's greatest players, remembers how the coach was into fitness. "He was fit himself and wanted his players to be fit. He always used to say, 'baseball is not going to make you fit but you have to be fit to play baseball. If you hit an inside the park home run you should be able to grab your glove run out to the field and make a diving play.'"

Russo recalled how the pre-season regime was dedicated to getting into shape.

"We did some crazy stuff in the gym. We didn't have a closed batting cage there. Coach used to throw batting practice in an open cage and baseballs were flying all over the small gym.

"He used to make us wear a mask. We had taped up socks. You would be flipping the sock baseball to a fellow just five feet in front of you and he would be taking full batting swings. All you would be wearing for protection was a chest protector and a mask. You would get pummeled. It was just Fitz being Fitz and teaching us baseball."

Greg Fonde played on Fitzpatrick's second and third teams in 1982 and 1983 and remembered the school's minimalistic weight room that was attached to an old wood shop area. The room might have been an auto tech room that had low tech Nautilus machines.

"Someone made an actual net batting cage that was suspended

from the ceiling," Fonde said. "There were ropes and pulleys. Coach would use sock balls. They were actually tube socks that were wrapped in white athletic tape."

Spring 1981 eventually arrived in Ardsley with a biting wind that blew unmercifully on the baseball diamond because of Ardsley's high elevation. That didn't matter to Coach Fitzpatrick. He was in heaven getting ready for his first season opener as a varsity coach.

For that first game and for nearly every other game of his coaching career, Coach Fitz would be the first one on the diamond.

It was 50 to 75 yards from Ardsley's locker room to the baseball diamond, a uniquely designed field.

"The old field was unique," Coach Fitz said. "The school's track was built around the entire baseball field. It wasn't the typical oval track. It had a weird shape. Centerfield was short. And that's interesting because that was my philosophy about hitting. I stressed hitting the ball up the middle. There were some home runs hit over those bleachers. I loved the field. I thought it was unbelievable."

Years after retiring, Coach Fitz still sang the praises of Joe Bucci, the groundskeeper and Joe Urbanowicz who nurtured his baseball diamond for all his coaching years.

Jeff Caldara, who started at shortstop for the '87 and '88 championship teams, also took delight in talking about the field.

"It was 330 feet down each line," he said. "It was about 360 in the gaps, totally legitimate. When it came to centerfield it was 330. That was where you were going to hit home runs. That plus being so high up. The high school was one of the highest points in the region.

"One thing great about the infield was that if it rained at 9 o'clock in the morning by 4 that afternoon we would be playing our games because it was so high and so windy."

Greg Fonde also recalled the irregular track around the field. "What was great about the field was that people who were there for track practice or mingling around the back of the school had an easy access to the field," he said. "All the kids who were practicing were in that vicinity."

Ardsley's diamond didn't have standard dugouts. The first and third base dugouts were slabs of concrete. "There was no fence in front of you," Fonde said. "You had to stay awake during the game."

Fans also got a bird's eye view of the games because they sat in a small set of bleachers close to the field behind a fence that was a few feet in back of the catcher.

While the track athletes didn't complain when balls cleared the fence and landed on the track, eventually somebody complained and Ardsley would finally build a new baseball field in another part of the school's campus. That's where the team plays today.

For the record, Coach Fitz's first 1981 varsity game was a loss. Five more losses followed before he chalked up his first victory. However, by season's end Fitzpatrick's team won the league title something the high school had never done before.

Leading the way for Fitzpatrick's first three seasons was shortstop Paul Murphy who Neil remembers fondly and would reconnect with many years later on Ardsley's baseball diamond. Murphy was something special, a particular favorite of Coach Fitz. He was not only Ardsley's best player at the time but also one of the best in Westchester County.

"Paul Murphy elevated us to a higher level of play," Fitzpatrick said. "If I didn't have Paul as my first shortstop who knows what would have happened."

In the early eighties Fitzpatrick's teams got better with each passing season and closer to the big prize, a state title.

Neil Fitzpatrick

Neil Fitzpatrick elected to Westchester Sports Hall of Fame in 2016.

4. RUBBER ARM MAN

At every Ardsley High School practice baseballs jumped off a batter's bat and landed somewhere, mostly in fair territory. Neil Fitzpatrick was delivering those pitches.

While most coaches were on the sidelines, at Ardsley Coach Fitz was busy throwing batting practice every day. And what a BP pitcher he was.

Batting against Fitz was like facing a pitching machine. His control was impeccable. He threw BP like no Westchester high school coach probably has ever thrown.

Neil threw BP because he enjoyed it. He also pitched for strategic reasons.

"I happened to like throwing batting practice partly because I was very good at it," Fitzpatrick said. "I wanted my players to have a field day with my meatball fastball. The whole idea was to give them confidence."

Neil prided himself on throwing batting practice better than anyone else. "I'm talking about anybody," he said. "I thought it helped our batters tremendously. I was proud that from one to nine in our lineup every single person was a solid hitter. There was no such thing as our number eight fellow being an automatic out. Our eighth batter might go four-for-four today.

"We had a reputation that we could hit. But I was equally as proud about our defense. We weren't a one-dimensional team. While it seemed like we spent all our time practicing hitting we spent a lot of time knowing how to steal a base, how to tag up, and how pitchers should cover first base.

But make no mistake Coach Fitz took batting practice personally. Throughout his coaching career he served an important and underrated role. He was entrusted with throwing to his players every single day before and during the season. Each pitch he threw, and there were hundreds of them daily, was expected to hit its intended location, with the resulting rocket shots zipping to each side of the protective netting near Neil.

Throwing BP might seem simple and easy to the average fan, but those coaches like Neil consider it an art form. As much as anything, Neil's pitching efforts contributed to the Panthers hitting success.

All Ardsley batters respected Neil's pitching prowess for its consistency, first and foremost, and his durability. Throwing all those pitches in just the right spot, and at just the right speed was all in his day's work. He knew he was doing a good job when his batters were hitting line drives back up the middle of the diamond. His arm hardly ever ached. The endless repetition was well worth it as all his players found their comfort zone. They loved his metronomic pace that enabled them to get their timing down pat.

Fitzpatrick's 1986 shortstop Billy Bakker remembers Fitzpatrick's pitching. He also talks about how Fitz's accessibility was something else.

"If we had a free period in school and Fitz was free, it wasn't out of the realm of possibility that he would be pitching us batting practice eighth period.

"He was the best batting practice pitcher I ever saw. I have an eleven year old son. The best thing I can do is pitch batting practice to him the way Coach Fitz threw to us.

"When Jeff Caldara set up a first annual Alumni Game in October 2016, Coach Fitz was there. There were scores of former players there as well. Fitz just pitched like it was the old days.

"I made a point. It was a choice between facing him or Jeff Caldara. I told Jeff that there was no way he was going to pitch me batting practice. I had to face Coach Fitz. I wanted Fitz to pitch in front of my son. I wanted my son Simon to watch this greatness. This guy is probably in his late sixties now and for me it was like being sixteen again. He just threw strikes right over the plate."

Mike Ferraguzzi who pitched relief and contributed mightily to two state titles said Fitz made practice fun. "He was out there throwing batting practice every single day. They called him 'rubber arm.' That was his nickname."

"When I threw batting practice my main motivation was to instill confidence," Fitzpatrick said. "I never wanted the pitchers on the team to throw BP because, naturally, they didn't want hitters teeing off on them. I on the other hand threw meatballs and if I could get the weakest hitter on the team to tease me about "drooling" to get an at-bat against me, I knew I was successful.

"I'm pretty sure there was no other high school team around that got as much live-arm batting practice as my teams. The pitching machines were ok if you didn't have a live-arm like mine. I feel blessed as a coach for having the ability and desire to be a good batting practice pitcher."

Neil once did have a regret about his batting practice prowess. His pitcher Todd Summer was also quite a hitter. The team was making fun about Fitzpatrick's pitching. Todd joined in the fun.

"Somehow I mustered up a high hard fastball that hit Todd. He was taken aback wondering how that could have happened. I got a chuckle out of it but for the next few games which happened to be our playoffs Todd struggled at the plate.

"I felt that my little chuckle was definitely not worth it. If you ask Todd today, I'm sure he would say that his slump had nothing to do with that practice session. But it points out how strongly I believe that a coach's job is to instill confidence. In this case, I came up short."

5. WHAT YOU DO IN PRACTICE YOU DO IN A GAME

What you do in practice you do in the game.

That's the most important lesson Neil Fitzpatrick ever took from his high school coach Hugh Kirwan. Coach Fitz adopted and followed it wholeheartedly throughout his entire coaching career. All his players bought into it for sure.

His philosophy was simple and yet so true. Practice as if it is a game and then the game will be like practice. That was Neil Fitzpatrick's mantra.

All Neil wanted to do was design the perfect practice. His goal was to have two hour practices and not a minute longer. He practiced what UCLA basketball coach John Wooden used to say, "If you can't do it in two hours, you're doing something wrong."

"I bought into that completely and tried to make my baseball practices simulate game situations," Fitzpatrick said. "The reason I would hit so many ground balls to infielders was that I wanted every possible hop that a ball could take to occur in practice.

"I always favored what I called live bat grounders over fungoes. If you're a second baseman and a coach keeps giving you grounders while looking at you that is very different from the slicing ground ball that comes after a late swing off a real fastball. So instead of fungoes, I got pretty good at letting our pitcher toss me meatballs. I could swing and direct the ball with all sorts of action to all of the infielders."

Practice plans and Fitzpatrick were synonymous. For years, he posted on the bulletin board what the practice would be. That came after he spent time devising how the practices would go.

Coach Fitz didn't spend much time talking. He spent time on repetition. He wouldn't bore his players with a half hour discussion about pickoff plays. But by the time the team played its first game each season, the players knew how to handle every situation. There would be no surprises.

"If you don't take your practice seriously you won't improve," he said. "And if during a game you treat the situation with too much seriousness, you won't be relaxed enough to perform.

"Early on, I believed that not coming through under pressure or choking was a moral issue. The best advice I ever got on the topic of choking came from my high school coach Hugh Kirwan. Kirwan told us that there is no such thing as choking if you give 100 percent."

Fitzpatrick's training rules for his teams were the same rules he got from Kirwan.

"He treated us like adults and told us, 'Don't ever do anything that would make you less than 100 percent for practice or a game. If you do, you are letting down your team.' I can remember after winning the first state championship I considered the season over. I'm positive the guys were celebrating in their hotel rooms afterwards. My only admonition was to be courteous, proud, and not too loud."

There were few things Fitzpatrick didn't take note of when it came to baseball preparation. That included even how to wear a baseball hat.

While Hall of Famer Ken Griffey Jr. wore his hat backwards during practice, Fitz wanted his players to wear their hats on straight all the time. According to Fitzpatrick, the world looks different when the brim of your hat is blocking out the sun.

Coach Fitz was a big believer in the game of pepper. His players loved it. Many high school teams don't use it at practice. It once was a common batting and fielding exercise and even a competitive game in baseball. One player hits brisk ground balls and line drives to a group of fielders who are standing around twenty feet away. The fielders throw to the batter who uses a short, light swing to hit the ball on the ground towards the fielders. The fielders field the ground balls and continue tossing the ball to the batter.

"We would play a game of errors where the hitter would pepper to three fielders," Fitzpatrick said. "He would stay at bat until the combined fielders caught 10 grounders in a row. You could become so good at pepper that you could start giving your fielders one-hoppers, two-hoppers or more.

"I tried to instill in all my hitters that when they were up at bat in a real game they should just pretend they were playing pepper and hitting a hard grounder to the pitcher. If you are successful you've got a base hit up the middle. Your mistakes would be line drive doubles in the outfield gap as well as home runs."

Tom Caldara remembers how Coach Fitz threw the most legendary batting practice. "He wanted you to put the ball in play and make the defense make a play. "Pepper the ball in. Slap it up the middle. When I was going up to the plate I was actually thinking about driving the ball up the middle which helped me keep a simpler shorter swing.

"When you think about hitting the ball up the middle what ends up happening is quite often you can be driving the ball to left field or to right center because you're keeping everything very contained.

"To this day when I coach or work with my son or daughter, I say, 'when in doubt, just hit it up the middle.'"

Fitzpatrick's practices were like clockwork. He would hit fungoes to one side of the infield. Someone else would hit to the other side. It was workmanlike. Ardsley High School probably took more infield groundballs than any team in the county.

"He wanted us to take so many ground balls so that we would see every single hop that our home field had to offer," Caldara said. Fitzpatrick's infielders had so many quality repetitions that come game time there was not a hop that they had not seen.

His players bought into this and would say, "keep them coming." They wanted to field difficult hops because they knew it was fun to make the play with their teammates watching.

There were very few things Fitz overlooked when it came to practice. He taught his pitchers how not to balk, how runners should take their leads when on first, second or third base.

He fostered attitudes unlike other Westchester high school baseball coaches. Whoever was at bat, he made sure the entire bench was visualizing a line drive for their teammate. Why? Fitz believed that when a batter senses this camaraderie, he does in fact do better.

An example of behavior that was very popular that Coach Fitz did not allow was something that looked cooperative but actually fostered negative thinking. It was getting your teammate's glove for him if he was on base when the third out of the inning was made. This way he wouldn't have to come into the dugout and he could wait for his teammate to bring him his glove.

"I wanted my player to be confident that he wasn't going to be stranded out there, and that he was indeed going to score because the batter would drive him home and then he could get his own glove, " Fitz said. "Why prepare for a negative thing?"

Fitz was always big on no surprises.

"I remember hearing that Brooks Robinson took 100 grounders every day to stay ready for his season," he said. "I didn't count the number of ground balls I hit in practice but I wanted it to be so many that there is not a bad hop you have not encountered. If, in practice, you see every possibility you will know that the game will be like practice. I also liked to hit grounders with a player pitching balls to me (not just lobbing the ball to myself) so that the fielders would get to see the ball coming off the bat just like in a game.

"You need to spend at least one solid practice (usually a rainy day indoor session because it can get tedious) going over every possibility that can happen. Start with nobody out and nobody on. The ball can be hit or bunted to any of the nine defenders and you want all nine players to know where they should go on each hit. Work your way up to bases loaded with two outs."

Neil never considered himself to be a great communicator. He thought teaching was more by example.

"I don't think I was a great pep talk guy," he said. "I think the kids knew where my heart was. They knew I wasn't a goofball or a nerd about baseball. I just loved the game. I think they got that."

They sure did. Billy Bakker played shortstop on Fitzpatrick's first state title team and remembers his practices.

"Our performance was all a function of him because of the way he was so organized and the way he practiced," Bakker said. "He played the game himself. So we respected him. We used to run in the hallways during the winter time. He would run with us. He wouldn't just sit there with a stick and yell at us. We gained a lot of respect from him. He was a terrific athlete."

C.J. Russo played for Coach Fitz and then coached 14 years at Ardsley High School with Jeff Caldara.

"Jeff and I used to sit in the dugout during our first couple of years of coaching under Fitz," Russo said. "Then Fitz handed the team over to us after two years when he retired. For the first four or five years Jeff and I would sit in the dugout and when we had to make big decisions, we would ask each other what would Fitz do right now.

"Practice mentality was what Fitz preached. Everything was written out. Everything was organized. If we were playing an intra-squad scrimmage he had every team evenly balanced. Our practices were exact sometimes even down to the language that Fitz used. That's how much of an influence he had.

"It was all about practicing hard and playing hard, keeping your mouth shut and letting your game speak for what you do day in and day out. He was one of those guys who loved hustle. He was intense."

Chris Presbyto, the centerfielder on Fitz's first state championship in '86, told a reporter that Fitz was not like other coaches. "He doesn't make us run. If he wants us to run, he runs with us."

Fitzpatrick remembers giving a speech somewhere along the lines where he mentioned his mom who raised his family. His dad had died at a young age.

"I remember thinking how our home was very disciplined. We had to get good grades. We couldn't curse. But there were a lot of laughs. In some ways, I thought that was my practices. There were certain violations. You couldn't wear your hat on backwards. But you could laugh your ass off if there was something funny."

Coach Fitz understood the motivation of each of his players. He didn't talk too much. He didn't lecture. But when he spoke and had something to say, it was important. His words were little nuggets and had value. Everyone knew that.

Tom Caldara recalls how baseball was so natural for Coach Fitz.

"As far as the game goes, it is hard to find a better guy when it came to fundamentals and doing the physical things the right way. But on top of that is being taught how to play the game the right way. Anything from your body language to sportsmanship to backing up bases."

Tommy Ferraguzuzi, Fitzpatrick's catcher on his '89 championship team, recalls that Fitzpatrick never questioned his pitch selection. "If you have to call the pitches for your catcher then you have the wrong catcher. That is how Fitzpatrick felt."

Ardsley's unequaled success in the eighties circles back to Fitz. He gave his players the chances and laid it out for them.

It was magical. For these young ballplayers it was all about being on Coach Neil Fitzpatrick's field in high school and having their friends and family watch them perform. Never again could they replicate what they got from Little League and high school, the beauty and innocence of playing the game for the love of the game.

6. RECOLLECTIONS ABOUT COACH FITZ

From childhood through his coaching days at Ardsley High School much of Neil Fitzpatrick's life was a baseball game. What was he like as a coach and as a man? I leave it to a few who played on his New York state championship teams to tell you. These are their recollections in their own words.

Jeff Caldara

At the end of the 2018 season, I finished my 21st year as head coach and 25th in the Ardsley system. I did one JV, three under Neil, and 21 as the head coach. Neil did 17 years as varsity head coach, and a total of 26 years, mix in jv, freshman.

With Coach Fitz if you worked hard and you proved you knew the game and how to play the game he would basically let you be.

Sometimes if things went on and he had to make a tweak here or there he would do it, but by and large he was a coach of repetition. In baseball that really fits the bill whether it's fielding grounders constantly or catching fly balls. He was a guy who was committed to that. If you did your job that was his strength. He would very rarely add anything because you were doing what you were supposed to do.

A lot of that is how I coach now. Some people don't understand that. They want people to be more demonstrative. If you worked hard and you did what you were supposed to do, Coach Fitz gave you the freedom as 16 and 17 year old boys that you never would have had.

He was the health teacher to many of his players. He mentioned that wasn't a strong point. He wasn't the most comfortable health teacher. But on the baseball field he had this little mini sarcasm that you didn't see in the health class. That allowed us to relate to him even more.

He wasn't that affectionate guy who was going to hug you and come up to you and give you life advice. But you knew he always had your back.

When we did something wrong we didn't feel guilty about letting him down. We felt guiltier amongst ourselves because we were so accountable to one another.

When it came to making a mistake coach never made you feel bad because he would never chastise you during a game. He would bring that up during practice. That was one of the great qualities of playing for him. You could play with this sense of relaxation. You knew that if you made a mistake he wasn't going to come flying at you and bombard you with anger.

I've been coaching Ardsley's baseball varsity for more than twenty years and Coach Fitz has impacted that coaching. I've incorporated things he did like first and foremost empowering the athletes.

I try to do as little talking as possible. I will go over what we need to do whether it is infield or outfield drills and then it is up to the players to make it happen. I think that is tremendously important for a kid at that age. I don't know how often that happens.

It is also my demeanor on the field. I can't be Neil. We are totally two different people. Once in a while I will raise my voice a little bit more than Neil did. But by and large I am very relaxed and very quiet during a game.

I also took his work ethic of being on time and letting the players know that they are accountable to their teammates. In 2017 we had 16 kids on the varsity baseball team. There are 400 boys in the school. The boys represented Ardsley High School in baseball and that is a pure privilege. That is something I always think about when I am coaching.

There is also the way Coach dealt with players. He was very consistent across the board. When he dealt with a C.J. Russo, a superior talent, and the 14th or 15th guy on the bench, he was pretty consistent in regards that one guy. The best player on the team would get 20, 30, 40 cuts at bat. The lowest guy on the team would get the same amount of reps. He knew that whether the youngster was going to get into the game or not, it was important that he felt part of the team.

Tom Caldara

Baseball was so natural for Coach Fitz. It is hard to find a better guy when it came to fundamentals and doing the physical things the right way. But on top of that is being taught how to play the game the right way. That was anything from your body language to sportsmanship to backing up bases.

He was all about learning to play the game the right way and teaching us always how to be the right type of person. His teaching fundamentals was for my money second to none. He gave you consistency and repetition that helped maximize your ability.

Coach Fitz did not micro manage. He let us play. He built to your strengths. He gave you the repetitions and then he let you run with it. He didn't over coach. He let us work through things and communicate amongst ourselves. I feel that is one of the keys to our success.

You have to be a person who is very confidant as a coach to let go of some control. That's what he did very often. He let us do what we were doing in the backyards for years. That translated into big games.

He was early for practice. He was so excited for practice. This is someone who you could tell absolutely loved the game. That was contagious. He could never get enough of it.

He had that specific gear on for practice and it looked like he was ready for a game because he had his stirrups pulled up high. He was ready to go in every practice like it was a game.

From time to time, he would pull us aside and have conversations with each of us. I knew that he was probing to make sure that we were doing the right thing off the field. He would give a brief speech at the end of a practice and before a big game. He would talk to us about appreciating the moment and also going home and getting some rest.

For me, it felt like someone who cared more about us and how we felt and being in the moment rather than the actual future outcome of the next game.

He had this quiet strength and confidence. He would prepare you and then let you go out on your own and apply what he prepared you for. You definitely didn't want to let him down particularly with the mental part of the game.

You didn't want to do something that was out of character of his team philosophy which was to play the game the right way. It was about sportsmanship, playing hard and staying humble. If you went outside those lines you knew that he wouldn't like that. You would do your best to stay within that world out of respect for him.

I remember we would mimic how he would hit fungoes. He is a little shorter than several of us. He would get excited. We would mimic his voice. "Hey let's go guys. Come on let's get it going. We're just standing around here." We would use that type of voice and speak a little more quickly but enthusiastically. It sounded almost child-like.

We did a physical copying of things he would do. In the school's bleachers at night you could hear someone imitating his voice. In a high pitched tone you would hear, "Pass me another beer." It sounded like he would say, "flip me a baseball." That imitation was done out of respect because we loved him.

Having seen Fitz over those years, I would say he didn't change one iota. That's a testament to him. He had a consistency in his character. Everything was very routine oriented. He had his beliefs about how to play the game the right way in terms of hustling and playing as a team player and being selfless. That was consistent all these years.

He did not communicate any additional pressure from my freshman year to my senior year. He was always the same which I think was so helpful to us and he would say, "What are we doing today to prepare so that we're better for tomorrow?"

Any pressure that was applied as the years progressed came from ourselves. I know personally as I got up to my junior and senior years in more of a leadership role, I felt that we had to win because I had an obligation to continue what the players before me started.

I wanted to win for them and win for the town. Whatever pressure was felt was self applied because we had this whole town behind us. We wanted to keep it going. We wanted those former players to come back and watch us keep the winning going. Pressure was definitely self applied.

C.J. Russo

Our success was all attributed to Fitz. He was a no holds bar kind of guy. He had his goofy moments at times but he never let his guard down.

Practice mentality was what Fitz preached. Everything was written out. Everything was organized. If we were playing an intra-squad scrimmage he had every team evenly balanced. Our practices were exact sometimes even down to the language that Fitz used. That's how much of an influence he had.

It was all about practicing hard and playing hard and keeping your mouth shut and letting your game speak for what you do day in and day out.

Coach Fitz was always the first one out to the field. There was no way a player was going to beat him out to the field after school. We had cement benches in the dugout. There wasn't a fence in front of the dugout. Fitz would be throwing a ball against the cement bench as we took ground balls.

When we came to practice he would throw two hours of batting practice. He had his back to us most of the time and we were working in the field. Billy Bakker and I were working on double plays. We were constantly working on defense.

That's the other thing that comes to mind. I read that during our '86 run of eight playoff games, we committed but one error. We turned double digits in double plays. We were constantly working on defense. Fitz always preached defense. No matter how good we hit the ball, we might have had a team batting average of something like .380, every reporter would ask about our hitting. Coach Fitz always deflected the conversation to how well the team played defensively.

Coach Fitz was intense. I got a chance to coach with him a little bit. He was the third base coach. He was in charge. When you were at bat he was in charge.

Back in those days there were no assistant coaches for us. When someone was slumping a little bit and we were feeling flat, Fitz would sneak over to the front of the dugout. He believed in mental telepathy. He would say to all of us, let's cheer this guy on and let's get him a hit. He believed in that. It would wake the bench up. We would start cheering and rooting for the guy who was at bat.

When we were in the field, he always stood towards the front end of the dugout nearest home plate. You could always find him there.

Another thing about Fitz was how he handled in-game adjustments. He just let you play. We were good. All of his coaching took place during practice. That is what he preached a lot of even when I was coaching with him. During the game you have to let guys play. I believe in that too. He let us play.

He used to say to us that every major leaguer takes at least 100 ground balls a day. Whether that's true or not I don't know. He probably made it up. He probably never read that anywhere but he believed in it.

He used to say a good way to take ground balls was to throw the ball up against the curb or the wall. Every day we came out for practice there he was waiting for us. He was throwing the ball against the cement bench.

We really worked hard at defense and Fitz believed in playing good defense. I remember days when we practiced playing the infield close up. Fitz would stand at home plate, even in the gym he used to do this. He would hit ground balls as hard as he could and we used to count how many we would field. His belief was to just knock the ball down and get the out.

I had a kid ask me once when I first started coaching and teaching, "Coach what do you want to do?" I was just out of college, painting houses. I replied, "I wanted to be Fitz." That meant coaching Ardsley baseball and having a great run. Eventually Jeff and I won a section championship.

Hitting is contagious. Good defense is contagious. And winning is contagious. When new people came in it just bred that winning atmosphere. We wanted to win again. Who didn't want to win again. It was such a great experience. And we demanded more out of guys who didn't think they had it. They produced.

Billy Bakker

I think the world of the guy. He's been a big impact on my life. I did love the game so much and in those games I focused as much as I could.

His practice was something that you repeated over and over and over again. Routine ground balls or double plays. Our performance was all a function of him because of the way he was so organized and practiced. He played the game himself. So we respected him.

We used to run in the hallways during the winter time. He would run with us. He wouldn't just sit there with a stick and yell at us. We gained a lot of respect from him. He was a terrific athlete. He was the best batting practice pitcher I had ever seen.

Our team was so loaded, so talented. All Coach Fitz needed to do was get us ready to play every day and not be complacent. I've seen plenty of teams who felt they could just walk out and win. That was what he was great at. Don't be complacent. Stay focused.

When there were times when we were down and we scored five or six runs, a lot of that had to do with him and his motivation. He would say, "You guys are fine, don't worry about it. You guys are going to hit. You know how to hit."

It was my pleasure playing for him. He was amazing.

Coach Fitz was never one to kind of share his thoughts. I think later on life he did more of that. He was our health teacher. He would pontificate and we would kind of kid him about it when he would talk about stuff. He had the buttoned up shirt and was always trying to do the right thing. So when a subject like sex education came up Fitz would turn red and we would always laugh. We knew it wasn't his personality. He wasn't comfortable talking about that but he had to talk about it because he was the health teacher.

Coach Fitz knew as much about baseball as any coach I played for. When I left Fitzpatrick it was all downhill.

Fitz was somebody who didn't fraternize with parents. He kept his distance. He was a teacher and we were the players. It was a big deal to play baseball in Ardsley. A part of our success too was that we were so enamored by those teams that came before us.

I idolized teams that featured Paul Murphy, Greg Fonde, and Bob

Wilmoth. When Paul Murphy played shortstop I was in eighth grade and people used to make fun of me. I would go grab his home runs. That tradition is something we took great pride in.

Ray DiMartino

The practice really was the preparation. The game was almost a formality. Fitz's practice was all in preparation, paying attention, watching for the unexpected, and knowing what you're going to do when the ball is hit to you. By the time the game came around your instincts took over. When you are 16-17, instincts that take over at that age are very uncommon.

Fitz's mantras were "All 21 outs" "Do it with two". Don't let your guard down until you get all 21 outs. The thing that really got his juices going was when we had two outs and nobody on base and we would score a run.

Mike Ferraguzzi

Fitz made practice fun. He was out there throwing batting practice every single day. You saw a guy who was youthful, enthusiastic and always talking. He only expected that you would do your best and that results would come.

He never put the pressure on that the team had to win. That never happened. He would say, "We're down by eight runs or something and let's see what we can do. That's it. That's all. Let's think about this inning." He kept grounded in the actual moment in the games. Practices were fun. He enjoyed it. During practices he was a kid like his players.

You always knew where you were going to go with the ball. You anticipated what was going to happen in the next play. Coach Fitz always had you thinking about that kind of stuff. What's going to happen if someone hits a single? You knew where to throw the ball.

Fitz is just such a wonderful guy and such a positive influence on all of us. His youthful enthusiasm and love of the game was absolutely wonderful. It was contagious. You always wanted to do well not only for yourself but for Fitz. You wanted to do your best for the guy. He was a very fair guy. He let you know when you weren't doing something right. And he wasn't wrong.

He took care of the players but he also had a great time. He was like a little kid out there playing with us. If you look at one of his speeches, he would say that one of the great thing about the team is that they always had a great sense of humor. At practice, if there was a slow big guy running, even if there weren't runners on first and second base, we would always turn a triple play. And Fitz thought it was the most hilarious thing.

As the teams evolved through the years, Fitz adapted to each club. I remember when I was a senior, we could mess around with Fitz. And years later Fitz would say how much he loved that.

He grew with the kids. In the beginning it was all business. I remember he was throwing BP and we would always throw the balls around the mound so that they would be easier to collect. A lot of times, I would try and throw a ball and one hop it, trying to hit the protective screen. A lot of times I would hit Fitz in the back of the leg. Fitz wouldn't say anything. He got. He knew it.

Folks would ask about winning four championships in a row. I would say, of course we're a dynasty, we won four in a row. Other people had a different opinion and I take that opinion now. You have four distinct teams with different players. That really isn't a dynasty. The only one who was dynastic was Coach Fitz since he was there consistently.

Tommy Ferraguzzi

Part of Coach Fitz's whole philosophy was to do the same thing every time the same way. I wouldn't say he would change. The only thing he said was, "This is a new team. Last year's team won the state championship. This year's team did not." He was always moving forward.

He was also ahead of his time. At practice everyone was always moving. He never had long practices. He would say, "If you can't do it in two hours then you are doing it wrong." He was so efficient with his time.

Brian Lepore

I remember his rubber arm. He was able to throw BP (batting practice). It was the best BP I ever saw. College coaches, nobody could throw BP like this guy threw BP. He was just a little machine.

It was right down the pipe every time with good spin on it. He would change speeds from the first batter to the last batter. He never tired out.

I used to really look forward to him throwing BP before a game. I wanted to get a few licks in before we went to a game. The funny thing was that he didn't care. If he threw you a pitch and you hit the first one right up the middle or a line drive, he would go, "You're good. That's it." You would get one swing of the bat and you would have to walk off.

1986

7. Loss Becomes Lesson Learned

A heart breaking loss in 1985 may have helped Ardsley win its first New York state title the following year.

That season ending 7-6 loss to Marlboro High School in a regional playoff game could have haunted the team and its fans for years. Or, maybe, just one year. Despite that loss, there are more than a few players from that era who say that the '85 team was as good as any of the four state championship clubs.

"We started the season 18-0," said George Phillips. "No other Ardsley team did that."

"When we lost in '85 I remember some parents being ticked off because they thought we should have won the title," Fitzpatrick said. "I was so happy to have won the sectional championship that year."

Then there was Coach Fitz's take on the loss. He never reflected on the negative. He just moved forward.

"That's the amazing thing about him," said Jeff Caldara. "He never brought that game up to my recollection. He treated each year as a different entity with a different collection of players.

"The goals might have been similar. He never spoke about the end goal. It was known within all of us. We knew we had the talent. Guys like C.J. Russo, Ray DiMartino and Brian Lepore, who were part of the '85 team that lost, made sure that it wouldn't happen again."

George Phillips, who was involved in that '85 game, said, "I don't know if it motivated me anymore because all I wanted to do was play ball.

"During that season once you start winning you don't want to lose, especially in '85 when we were 18-0 and then lost to North Salem. It was tough. I wasn't a main component of that pitching staff. The funny thing is that the two years I played for the varsity we were 48-3. I had all three losses. All of the losses were in relief. Every game I started I completed and won."What might have haunted Ardsley players and fan base was how the Panthers lost to Marlboro High School in that '85 regional playoff game at Brewster High School. With a 22-1 record and a five run lead with only three outs left in the game most everyone thought Ardsley would win.

Then Ardsley was saddled with pitching problems. Mike DiMartino walked the bases loaded to start the seventh. Marlboro went on to score six times en route to a shocking 8-7 win.

DiMartino had only given up four singles through six innings. Then he simply lost control. After walking the bases loaded, he hit one batter to drive in one run and walked another to drive in another run.

Coach Fitzpatrick saw enough. He called on relief pitcher George Phillips with the bases loaded and none out. Phillips threw a fastball to Marlboro's second hitter in the order who smacked an opposite field triple to right, clearing the bases and tying the game 7-7. A sacrifice fly to left drove in the winning run.

More than three decades after that fateful inning, Phillips said, "It was a good fastball and I threw it by him. He hit one of those cap jobs off the end of his bat. It got over the first baseman's head and had so much spin on it that it spun to the right hand corner of the field and cleared the bases. The next batter hit a sacrifice fly and there was a bang-bang play at the plate and I thought he was out. But the ump called him safe."

After all these years, Ardsley shortstop Billy Bakker remembers the game better than most.

"We won the section in 1985 and played in Brewster," he said. "I live in Carmel and passed by Brewster High School at least once a week for nineteen years. We had a 6-2 lead going into the seventh inning. Ed DiMartino was pitching. He was our best pitcher. He was all section. His brother was catching. For whatever reason he just lost all control.

"With that 6-2 lead we were in the dugout jumping up and down thinking that we had won this game and that we were going to miss school the next day because the following game was going to be in Long Island at Hampton Bays.

"It was one of those situations where in our heads we had the game won already. We didn't focus that we had to get three more outs.

"It was a heart breaking loss. From that day forward, all of us on that team dedicated ourselves not to let that happen again. That loss stuck in our minds every game we played in '86. I think that loss contributed to us winning the '86 championship.

"The two brothers, Ray's twin brothers, Ed and Mike DiMartino and our catcher Andy Carson were seniors. They had to suffer through that heart breaking loss. On top of that, they attended our game and watched us win the 1986 state championship.

"I'm not somebody who had taken that championship and told everyone at cocktail parties that I've won a state title. I've been very humbled by the experience. I don't talk about it a lot with people. I don't think people really care except for my teammates. I felt so bad for Ed, Mike and Andy who didn't win the title.

"The '85 team was better than the '86 team. I believe we had to lose that season to win the state championship in 1986. Our title was one of the contributing factors for the other three titles. It was something that was part of an Ardsley mystique."

"All 21 Outs" soon became the mantra for Ardsley baseball.

8. BOYS OF '86

There was good reason Coach Neil Fitzpatrick wasn't astounded during the early weeks of practice in 1986 about how smooth the boys moved. They simply knew each other's every move since Little League days when they first started playing ball together.

Entering the '86 season Ardsley had few weaknesses. There wasn't one sophomore on the team. That would change. Every year after that, '87, '88 and '89, Coach Fitz went to his JV coach and requested three players who had worked hard to come up to the varsity to experience play in the sectionals.

Despite graduating four starters from the 1985 22-2 team, the Ardsley Panthers remained the same at key positions up the middle. The combination of second baseman C.J. Russo and shortstop Billy Bakker was among the best in the county. John Feinauer, a right-hander who finished 8-0 in '85 anchored a pitching staff that included George Phillips and Chris Presbyto, a left-hander.

Phillips worked hard that winter before the season began. At lunch time he would go into the school's gymnasium and throw pitches against a mat for 40 minutes. The more he threw the stronger he became. He also added a slider to his repertoire. Little did he know how much Coach Fitz would rely on him during the '86 season in so many different ways.

There may have been players who hit the ball more often than George, but nearly everyone in Westchester County agreed that Phillips, Ardsley's 6-1 215 pound slugger, hit it further than any other schoolboy. Coach Fitz shifted Phillips from first to third in '86 when he wasn't going to pitch. The coach didn't expect any drop-offs from his '85 stats – .470 batting average, 10 home runs, 38 RBI.

A battle early on was waged for the fourth pitching spot between juniors Ray DiMartino and Chris McNerney.

Phillips and Presbyto, a center fielder, were expected to provide most of the team's power. Sean McQuigan, the right fielder, hit over .350 in '85. Mike Corelli, the left fielder, was the other returning starter. Brian Lepore, a first baseman whose bat impressed Fitzpatrick in '85, forced the move of Phillips to third base, and junior Scott Minchak became the Panthers new catcher.

As the season opener got closer, Coach Fitzpatrick stood near the dugout watching the boys warm up. Potential lineups went through his mind.

Crouching behind the plate was catcher Scott Minchak. His teammates described him as someone who refused to lose. Besides catching, he was quite a pitcher with movement on his fastball. He threw a little sidearm. Pitchers also loved to pitch to him since he had a great arm and runners didn't take too many liberties.

Scott was a terrific teammate who cheered for everybody. When the team was down and needed to be picked up, Scott was the club's vocal leader. He also loved to fix things including the team's backstop.

At the third base hot corner was Ray DiMartino. He was Ardsley's No. 9 hitter but on any other team in Westchester County he would have most likely been a No. 4 or 5 hitter. Ray did it all. He was also a character, a jokester, who kept everyone loose.

Manning first base was Brian Lepore, a hardnosed player. He was a gamer who took a football mentality to the baseball diamond. He took great pride in playing defense and didn't mind if his infielders threw the ball in the dirt to him. He wanted to make a pick.

Brian Lepore and his swipe tag at first base were synonymous. He picked that play up from New York Met star Keith Hernandez. Brian would just slap the tag as hard as he could down on the runner and get the ball right back to the pitcher. If you were going to take a lead and there was a throw to first Brian was going to make you pay the price every time.

Scooping up balls at shortstop was Billy Bakker, a teammate who loved to practice. He was professional about his approach to the game. He was a 6 footer who weighed 170 pounds wet, who didn't lift weights and, unlike many of his teammates, didn't play football. Billy broke his leg in day camp when he was ten years old. He also was born with a bone cyst in his left femur and didn't know that until he broke his leg sliding. He had surgery and was told that if he wanted to play baseball he couldn't play football.

Out in right field, Coach Fitz watched Shaun McGuigan show off his throwing arm by firing bullets back to the infield. Whenever he picked the ball up at the fence he let it rip. When the ball came out of his hand it had some pop on it. One of his throws saved a game and pretty much Ardsley's season in '86. Throughout his high school career Shaun was a top notch hitter in hit and run situations as a left-handed batter who was adept at hitting to the opposite field.

In centerfield shagging balls was Chris Presbyto. Nicknamed CP, Presbyto batted left-handed, had a classic swing and hit for power. Besides playing the outfield, Chris pitched for Coach Fitz and threw plenty of strikes. His infielders knew that they would have to play defense since Chris didn't overpower people.

Presbyto was a very even keel guy and led by example. A sense of humor was part of his personality. He would make up funny stories about professional athletes. For example, if you were sitting in a bar and Dallas Cowboys defensive lineman Randy White walked in, Chris would ask whether you thought you could beat him up.

Chris was one of several players who hit .400 during the season but may have fallen under the radar.

Over in left field, Fitzpatrick watched the strongest fellow on the team, Mike Corelli. Mike loved the weight room and brought his work ethic to the team. He was a contact hitter and throughout the season made some great throws home. When the game was on the line Coach Fitz may not have had a better hitter than Corelli.

Out on the pitching mound Fitzpatrick kept an eye on two of his aces, John Feinauer and George Phillips.

Big John Feinauer, all of 6' 6", played an integral part in Ardsley's '86 season. He had issues throwing strikes early on. That's when there may have been a little bit of a lull in the infield. Coach Fitz would gather his infielders and tell them that we're going to need John to perform well, so let's pick him up. When John threw strikes he was lights out. He was intimidating because of his size and delivered some big game performances throughout his career.

George Phillips got his turn on the mound in '86. The best thing you could say about George was that he was a gamer. He loved to practice and practice hard. Day in and day out he came to practice ready to play.

Throughout his career, Ardsley fans knew they were going to get the best out of George. He was the team's workhorse. He started game after game for a while. No matter how bad his arm hurt, he just said, "Give me the ball Fitz, I'll be on the mound."

George knew what he didn't want to see as a hitter. That helped him as a pitcher going up against some of the better batters in the county. He was also one of the better home run hitters in the county.

Coach Fitz's eyes finally turned to one more player. He looked out towards second base and focused on C.J. Russo, a five-foot five-inch dynamo who could do it all. He made the varsity as a sophomore. C.J. was intense, old school, practiced hard and took the game seriously. He had great speed, a sure-handed glove, and was a powerful leadoff hitter. Using a short batting stroke he hardly ever struck out. In '86 Russo hit .506 and stole 15 bases. Coach Fitzpatrick said that Russo might have been the greatest athlete Ardsley ever produced.

The 1986 season was about to get underway.

9. RUSSO, PHILLIPS STIR QUITE A ROW

On a cold April 4 Ardsley High School opened the season at the Irvington Hudson River Baseball Tournament, an event Ardsley had won three times, in '82, '83, and '85.

John Feinauer and George Phillips combined to pitch five innings of no-hit ball against Hastings High School before the game was called after the fifth inning because of darkness. Ardsley picked up its first win of the season, 11-1.

This opening day win was a prelude for what was in store for many Ardsley opponents all season long, many Ardsley runs in nearly every game.

Every one of the Panthers' nine batters drove home at least a run against Hastings, with C.J. Russo and Scott Minchak each knocking in two. Russo's two-run double in the second inning highlighted Ardsley's seven-run rally. Minchak and Ray DiMartino both went 2-for-3 for Ardsley, for the school's first win of the season. Phillips went 2-for-4.

The next day George Phillips' long winter workouts started paying off. The senior right-hander struck out 12 batters in another 11-1 victory, this time over Sleepy Hollow in the championship game at Irvington's Memorial Park. For the second consecutive day Ardsley had 18 hits and for the second straight day did not commit an error.

Over the winter Phillips took a pitching course and he learned how to use more of his whole body while pitching. He now had a leg kick and wouldn't tire as quickly as he did in '85. He also started showing indications of overcoming another problem he suffered as a junior.

He walked just three batters.

In the fourth inning, Mike Corelli hit a three-run home run over the center field fence. Chris Presbyto, who went 3-for-4, with a walk and three RBI, brought home two runs with a long triple to right-center field in the fifth.

As a whole, the Panthers looked as good, if not better, than the team that advanced to the Southeast Regional final the previous season.

Two days later, in the first game of the Ardsley Tournament Phillips allowed two runs and two hits in the opening inning and then pitched hitless ball over the next six to shut down the Bronxville Broncos. C.J. Russo, Sean McGuigan, Chris Presbyto and Phillips all had 3 hits. Phillips also had 3 RBI, as well as 10 strikeouts.

Ardsley's next game against Rye Neck was one Coach Fitz called dramatic and perfect footage for a highlight film. He described it as high drama and the best that schoolboy baseball can offer.

On center stage were two of the best players in Westchester County, pitcher Chuck Taylor of Rye Neck and free-swinging George Phillips of Ardsley.

Taylor was one strike away from a 9-7 victory. One swing later, Phillips was in the spotlight with a grand-slam home run to the farthest reaches of left field. Ardsley added two more runs and eventually hiked its record to 4-0 after beating Rye Neck 13-9.

After six innings Rye Neck led 9-7. But when the first three Ardsley batters in the seventh walked, the Rye Neck coach summoned Taylor to the mound. He struck out the first batter, retired the next on an infield pop and got two quick strikes on Phillips.

One pitch and one out and the game would be over. That's when Taylor came in with a low outside fastball. Phillips went down and got it, fully extending his arms as he drove the ball over the fence with the game winning home run.

Sports fans throughout Westchester were now taking note about Phillips. In his next outing he upped his record to 3-0 in Ardsley's 11-1 win over Croton. Brian Lepore went 2-for-4 and knocked in three runs. Phillips struck out seven while giving up just one earned run. In 21 innings of pitching that was only the third earned run

George gave up. The game also marked the end of Phillip's 26-game hitting streak.

In game after game Ardsley continued to score double digit runs. No one seemed able to stop the Panthers. The team exploded for 10 runs in the third inning to beat Conference C guest Irvington, 14-3, to extend the Panthers' unbeaten streak to 6-0. John Feinauer got the win pitching 5 innings of six-strikeout seven-walk ball to pick up his second win.

When early season stats came out on April 18, George Phillips was fourth in the county with 12 RBI and tied for second with a 3-0 pitching record.

Eight days later Ardsley's six game winning streak came to an end at the hands of Pelham High School. Gary Scott's two out single in the bottom of the seventh was bobbled by Ardsley's leftfielder Mike Corelli allowing Pelham to score for a 10-9 victory in the championship game of the Ardsley Baseball Tournament. Phillips gave up the winning run. This would be Ardsley's only loss of the season.

Two days later the Panthers took out that loss on Irvington in winning 13-5.

The following day left fielder Mike Corelli and catcher Scott Minchak ended the game in spectacular fashion as Ardsley improved to 8-1 in beating Croton 4-2.

With two outs in the seventh and a Croton runner on second, Corelli charged a single in left field on one bounce and came up firing in throwing a strike to Minchak at the plate. The umpire looked for a moment and then pulled back his fist. "He's out!" Game over.

Ardsley's double digit run scoring wins kept piling up. In back to back games against Pleasantville High School the Panthers won 22-1 and 20-2. In the first game, Chris Presbyto's two home runs paced Ardsley to its ninth victory of the season.

Phillips and Ray DiMartino cracked homers and combined for 9 RBI. Sean McGuigan and Luigi Assente each drove in two runs. John Feinauer picked up the win in allowing only two hits while striking out five.

Two days later against Pleasantville again Sean McGuigan, Mike

Corelli and George Phillips had three hits apiece. On the mound George was his usual self. He gave up three hits in seven innings while striking out 12 and walking four. Ardsley remained undefeated in Conference C Central play with a 6-0 record.

Throughout his coaching career, Coach Fitz prided himself in having the lower part of his batting order produce. This year would be no different. Through May 4, Scott Minchak, the No. 8 batter in the lineup was hitting .411. Ray DiMartino batted ninth and was hitting .461. The lineup looked like a murderers' row. Leadoff hitter C.J. Russo was batting .450. He was followed by George Phillips .350, Mike Corelli .405, Bill Bakker .324 and Brian Lepore .282.

A unique batting situation was also helping Ardsley. The team's first three batters in every game were C.J. Russo, Shaun McGuigan and Chris Presbyto. They were all lefties. Lefty hitters are almost always faster getting down to first base. Russo and McGuigan were lightening.

By early May teams hadn't found an answer to stop Ardsley's big bats. On May 6, four Ardsley home runs, including three-run shots by Russo and Presbyto powered the 11-1 Panthers to a 18-4 win over Briarcliff High School. Presbyto finished with six RBIs while John Feinauer picked up the win.

Two days later Briarcliff lost again to Ardsley. This time it was 6-1. George Phillips hurled a three-hitter with eight strikeouts. He also homered in picking up his sixth win. Ardsley improved to 12-1. Mike Corelli had 2 hits and 2 RBIs while Brian Lepore added a two-run triple.

The long ball was Ardsley's specialty. Against Edgemont Ardsley won 12-1. George Phillips drove in three runs with a 2-for-5 performance that included a three-run homer, while Bill Baker knocked in two runs in a 3-for-5 effort. Chris Presbyto won his second game of the season.

The bad news for Edgemont was that it had to face Ardsley again. The outcome was no different. Ardsley won 15-5 with Phillips hitting two two-run home runs and winning pitcher Ray DiMartino smashing a 3-run shot. Phillips' four RBIs brought his season total to 30 and the two home gave him seven for the season.

Phillips wasn't the only offensive star for Ardsley. C.J. Russo was 3-for-4 with three stolen bases and one RBI and Sean McGuigan was 3-for-5 with three stolen bases and three runs scored. DiMartino's win put him at 3-0 for the season.

Valhalla High School was next on Ardsley's calendar. This was the season's first meeting of these previously undefeated WICC-Central teams. The outcome was never in doubt.

Bill Bakker hit a grand slam home run to cap an 11-run rally in the fifth inning. Ardsley won 15-1.

Ardsley continued its impressive combination of pitching, defense and opportunistic hitting in taking sole possession of first place. The win ended Valhalla's 13-game win streak as George Phillips scattered two hits and five walks while striking out nine batters to earn his seventh victory of the season.

Two days later, Ardsley asserted itself as the premier team in Conference C-Central by hitting six home runs in a 22-5 victory at Valhalla. Ardsley, 16-1 overall and 12-0 in the league, hit the home runs off five Valhalla pitchers. Second baseman C.J. Russo led Ardsley with two home runs and five RBIs.

"Russo is so strong for someone his size," Fitzgerald told the *Gannett Westchester Newspapers.* "I think he is outstanding. He's fast. He hits for consistency. He is just one great player."

Apart from Russo's two home runs, the Panthers got homers from Brian Lepore, George Phillips, Billy Bakker and Scott Minchak. Ardsley's Mike Corelli didn't hit any home runs, but he drove in four runs on three doubles. The Panthers had 17 hits with John Feinauer picking up his fifth win of the season.

"It was like batting practice and they don't need any practice," said Valhalla coach Jim Grieco in that same interview.

Westchester high school baseball stats through May 16 told Ardsley's story. George Phillips was third in the region with 29 RBIs. Chris Presbyto was seventh with 26 while C.J. Russo was 12th with 22. Phillips also was seventh in the area in pitching with a 7-1 record and Feinauer was 15th at 5-0.

Next up was North Salem. George Phillips hurled a two-hitter and helped his own cause with an RBI triple as visiting Ardsley edged

North Salem 2-1 in an Conference C- Central showdown.

Phillips' triple drove in Chris Presbyto who led off the fourth inning with a single. Phillips came in to score when Billy Bakker struck out on a pitch which eluded the catcher. This was one of the few games Ardsley was kept under double figures in runs scored in a game.

Presbyto Saves Ardsley, 10-3, headlined the *Gannett Westchester Newspapers.* Presbyto in relief survived a bases-loaded fourth inning North Salem rally and hit a three-run home run to give host Ardsley a 10-3 win. Ardsley was now 19-1 and completed a perfect 14-0 WICC-Central season.

Sports fans in the metropolitan New York area were now taking note about this small Westchester high school and its exploits on the baseball diamond.

On Sunday, May 25, Larry Cole's story in the *NY Daily News* was headlined,

Russo, Phillips Stirring Quite a Row At Ardsley and the story read:

The 1927 Yankees, one of baseball's best all-time great hitting team for whom the label "Murderers' Row" was originally coined, had nothing statistically on the 1986 Ardsley team.

Whereas that outstanding Yankee team had five .300-plus hitters including Babe Ruth and Lou Gehrig, Ardsley boasted a batting order composed of nine players hitting about .300.

Through Ardsley's first 18 games, here's the awesome group: leading off, second baseman C.J. Russo, 484; right fielder Sean McGuigan, 355; center fielder Chris Presbyto, .444; third baseman-pitcher George Phillips, .440; left fielder Mike Corelli, .409; shortstop Bill Bakker, .327; first baseman Brian Lepore, .339; catcher Scott Minchak, .327 and DH-third baseman Ray DiMartino, .387.

The bulk of the damage has been handed out by Russo, on base a minimum of three times a game, and Phillips, who had hit eight home runs and had driven in 35 runs.

Coach Neil Fitzpatrick at the time was reluctant to hand out too much praise and said his 17-1 team wasn't unusual. But when *New York Daily News* sports writer Larry Cole pressed, however, he admitted that no previous Ardsley team had compiled those awesome statistics.

Ardsley was carrying a team batting average of more than .380 and the club reached double figures in 14 of its 18 games while averaging 12.7 runs per ballgame.

Ardsley was never more devastating than in its two games against Valhalla, unbeaten in league play prior to that meeting. In two games, Ardsley blasted Valhalla by scores of 15-1 and 22-5.

Fitzpatrick, by now, was singing the praises of Ardsley defensive play. He rated his team's defense as being even more important than its batting. He knew the Panthers were making all the plays in the field, especially in the infield, paying special tribute to the double play combination of Bakker and Russo.

"These two have been playing together for a few years and work together beautifully," Fitzgerald said at the time. "And Russo turns double plays like a major leaguer."

Benefiting of all this were Ardsley's pitchers. John Feinauer had won all five of his decisions; Phillips was 8-1 while Presbyto was 3-0 and DiMartino was 1-0.

10. A TIME TO TEACH

Going into Westchester County's Class C Winners' Bracket quarterfinals, opposing players and coaches knew that Ardsley's baseball team was good.

Rye Neck High School lost to Ardsley earlier in the season and now would get another crack at the Panthers. They would soon find out that the result would be no different the second time around.

George Phillips hurled a five-hitter while his teammates hit four home runs in a 14-3 win. Phillips didn't allow a hit until the fourth inning and struck out seven batters to win his seventh game in eight decisions.

Ardsley, the tournament No. 1 seed at 20-1, characteristically ran away scoring 11 runs in the first three inning.

Billy Bakker hit two homers, including an inside-the-park grand slam and Chris Presbyto and Ray DiMartino hit two-run homers.

Bakker's first home run was the most unusual. With the bases loaded in the first inning, he hit a high grounder to shortstop that bounced off the lip of the infield and darted into the outfield. When the center fielder's diving try failed, the ball rolled to the fence and Bakker circled the bases.

"With that grand slam I got a fastball right over the outside of the plate," Bakker recalled. "Back in '86, especially in May and June Ardsley's infield was very hard. It was almost like Astroturf.

"The shortstop was ready to catch it and it went right over his head and darted to the outfield. I remember the centerfielder diving to try and stop the ball. He didn't get it and it rolled all the way to the wall.

I beat the throw home."

After crossing the plate Bakker soon had a confrontation with Coach Fitz who let Bakker know that he had done something wrong.

"In the heat of battle I hit that inside the park home run off of Chuck Taylor who everyone was talking about," said Bakker who admitted to having a bit of a temper. "I touched home plate and was yelling at Taylor. Fitz grabbed me and said 'If you ever do that again you'll never play on this team again.'

"I calmed down and from that day forward I never said a word. I let my play do the talking. Coach Fitz was very helpful to me in that way. He never called anybody out. In my particular situation, he sat me down later on the end of the bench when I cooled off. He came up to me and said, 'No that's not the way you play. That's not a classy move.' He would not tolerate us ragging on the other team. None of that ever happened again."

With that win against one of Westchester's top hurlers Ardsley then took on Blind Brook under a searing noonday sun. The Panthers unleashed a 22-hit assault and overpowered Blind Brook High School, 22-6, in the semi-final round of the Section 1 Class C baseball tournament. That win meant Ardsley had a chance to host Eastchester for the championship of the winners' bracket.

Against Blind Brook Ardsley scored eight runs in the first inning, sending a total of 12 batters to the plate to quickly put the game out of reach. Junior second baseman C.J. Russo led the attack with a home run, a triple, double and six RBIs. Russo now boasted a league leading .513 batting average.

The 21-1 Panthers got a strong performance from winning pitcher Chris Presbyto, who left after three innings with Ardsley leading 12-3. Presbyto, 4-0, struck out six and allowed three hits.

Scott Minchak, who started the game at catcher, relieved Presbyto and retired the next nine batters in a row before Ray DiMartino replaced him in the top of the seventh. Minchak also chipped in with a home run, double, and two RBIs while DiMartino went 3-for-4 including a triple and two doubles.

Two days later, Ardsley played one of its most challenging games of the season. After it was over Ardsley coach Neil Fitzpatrick called it a "classic game". This Section 1 Class C winners' bracket game against Eastchester certainly was that.

The game wasn't decided until the eighth inning when Eastchester's centerfielder dropped Ray DiMartino's line drive allowing the winning run to score in Ardsley's 5-4 victory.

"I was just trying to hit it hard," said DiMartino, who sent a fastball towards right-center field. The error, with runners on first and second, was the game's only fielding miscue.

For seven innings Eastchester's Brandon Walsh and Ardsley's George Phillips dueled. The Panthers tied the game 4-4 in the bottom of the seventh when C.J. Russo, the leadoff batter doubled, advanced to third on a sacrifice bunt, and scored on Presbyto's long fly ball to left field.

The loss dropped Eastchester to Class C Losers' Bracket and a game against Blind Brook which Eastchester won. All Ardsley needed to do was win one of two possible games to earn the trip to the Southeast Regional semi-finals.

A Saturday rain moved Ardsley's game against Eastchester to Sunday. This time a pair of home runs from the bottom of the batting order gave Ardsley an 8-6 win and its second consecutive Section 1 Class C baseball title.

Scott Minchak, the Panthers eighth batter, hit a three-run homer over the left field fence in the bottom of the fourth inning. Batting ninth in the order Ray DiMartino homered deep to center with one on in the bottom of the sixth.

Minchak's blow, which unknotted a 2-2 tie, provided enough runs for the junior hurler to pick up his first varsity win after throwing four strong innings. It was his first start of the season. Minchak was replaced by George Phillips who closed out the final three innings.

Minchak rewarded his coach for the faith he showed in him. "The first indication Scott gave me that he could do the job was last year when I saw him pitch on the JV level," said Coach Fitz in a *Gannett Westchester Newspapers* interview. "He showed me he definitely could do it when he pitched the last three innings and got nine quick outs in our win against Blind Brook. Also, I wanted to use him because Eastchester had never seen him pitch."

Minchak's battery mate was the Panthers' No. 1 utility player, Cy Richardson, another junior who played in the infield, outfield and behind the plate.

"I used to catch Scott when we both played in little league," said Richardson in that same interview.

Eastchester had tied the score in the fourth inning. The damage could have been worse if Richardson had not thrown out Eastchester's leadoff batter who was trying to steal second.

"I saw that the runner had a big lead at first and I really wanted to call a pitchout but we needed the strikes. When the runner left, our first baseman yelled 'running' and I just got up and threw it to second," said Richardson.

Ardsley 23-1 played solid defense that resulted in errorless baseball. The Panthers collected only five hits, three belonging to DiMartino and Minchak.

By early June three of the county's top ten RBI producers were Panthers. Phillips had 32, followed by Presbyto with 31 and Russo with 30. Phillips was tied for the county lead in home runs with 9.

In the *Daily News* Golden Twenty poll Ardsley held down the sixth spot in the metropolitan New York area. And when 72 of Westchester's Section 1's finest baseball players were honored at the Rye Golf Club, Fitzpatrick, Class C Coach of the Year, said what he liked about his club was its balance where everyone picked up the slack. If the 3-4-5 hitters weren't hitting, then the 7-8-9 guys were.

11. SWEET REVENGE

Call it sweet revenge. Call it payback. Call it reprisal.

Ardsley waited a year for a chance to avenge its Southeast Regional final loss to Marlboro High School in '85.

This time Ardsley won convincingly. The Section 1 champions continued on the "Road to Little Falls" where the New York State Public High School Athletic Association baseball finals would be held by defeating Section 9 champion Marlboro, 9-3, in the Southeast Regional semifinals at Monroe-Woodbury High School in Orange County.

The Panthers avenged the previous year Southeast Regional final loss to Marlboro by combining opportunistic hitting and base running, defense, and a solid effort by pitcher John Feinauer.

Feinauer, who had not pitched in post-season play because of recurring control problems, scattered seven walks and five hits before yielding to George Phillips, who retired the side in the seventh inning to nail down the win.

"I've been trying to find new ways to warm up and get my control," Feinauer told the *Gannett Westchester Newspapers* after the game. "It's like a haunting thing. If I spread out the walks I can go a long way. I let them hit the ball and the defense did the job."

Last year, Marlboro won an 8-7 ball game by scoring four runs with two out in the seventh inning. Phillips relieved during that inning and was the victim of a line drive inside first base that turned into a bases clearing triple.

Double plays in the third, fourth and fifth innings helped Feinauer escape potential jams while earning him his sixth win without a loss.

It had to make Phillips feel good when he got Ardsley's scoring started with a two-run home run in the first inning, a shot over the short left field fence. The Panthers scored three more times in the second and fourth innings and once in the third.

The second inning rally was highlighted by a bizarre play caused by Marlboro first baseman's mental lapse. With two out and Scott Minchak on first base, Ray DiMartino, hit a dribbler in front of the plate. The Marlboro catcher threw wildly to first base, pulling the first baseman off the bag. When the first baseman tried slapping DiMartino with a tag, the ball broke loose and ended up in short right field.

As the first baseman argued the play with the first base umpire, Minchak raced home and DiMartino ended up at third. Sean McGuigan later tripled past a drawn-in center fielder for two more runs.

All season long it was easy to overlook Ardsley's good defense what with a lineup packed with .300 hitters and batters who hit homers with reckless abandon. That's why perhaps the most important combination of teammates on Ardsley's field day in and day out was the second baseman and shortstop who worked together seamlessly for seven innings.

They knew where the other was positioned, and learned each other's rhythm, strengths and weaknesses. They trusted that their partner backed them up on missed plays, and knew without looking that they would be there when they fielded a grounder and turned to start the double play.

The core of the Panthers' defense all year was the double play combination of C.J. Russo at second and shortstop Billy Bakker. The pair combined for eight double plays during the season, including two in the Marlboro victory. Russo was also the middle man on a double play involving third baseman Phillips in that game.

Going into their senior year, the pair had been playing together since their days in Little League. They also played summer ball together, in addition to the time spent on the Panthers' junior varsity.

"We've been playing almost all our lives together," Russo told the

Gannett Westchester Newspapers after the Marlboro win. "We know each other's moves. He knows what I'm going to do and I know what he's going to do."

For years the pair spent endless hours in batting practice honing and perfecting their location and their pivots and improving the feel they had for each other's play.

"We really work hard on it," said Bakker in that interview. "We just work together so well."

In the Marlboro win, they each had a chance to execute their pivot. With none out in the fourth inning, Russo scooped up a slow bouncer and flipped it to Bakker, who threw a strike to first baseman Brian Lepore. In the following inning Russo turned his third double play of the game when Bakker ranged into the hole to his right to come up with a sharp shot.

"It's the old cliché, practice makes perfect," said Bakker. "This is the year we perfected it."

Years later, Bakker said, "C.J. and I practiced a lot. That's something Coach Fitzpatrick took pride in and made us do which made practices like the games. When we had batting practice, we were always in our fielding positions. We weren't goofing off. C.J. and I were constantly playing the positions. That's really where we practiced the double play. We perfected it in that '86 season."

12. ROAD TO THE FINAL FOUR

With one more win Ardsley would be on its way to the state's final four.

On June 10, George Phillips, pitching for the third time in as many days with nearly a dead arm, hurled a two-hitter as the Panthers defeated Section 11's Hampton Bays of Long Island, 4-2, in the '86 Class C Southeast Region final at Mahopac.

"I can't lift my arm," Phillips said after striking out two of four batters in the seventh inning. "It's not as bad as it was earlier. I had nothing in my arm. It was just hanging," he told the *Gannett Westchester Newspapers.*

Phillips walked seven batters and stranded four runners in scoring position in the fifth and sixth innings. He walked the bases loaded in the sixth but escaped when catcher Scott Minchak and first baseman Brian Lepore picked the runner off first.

Coach Fitz was waiting for one more batter to remove Phillips. George's fatigue began to concern Fitz in the fourth inning. But George was still throwing strikes and hung in there.

Ardsley overcame a 2-1 deficit by scoring three runs in the fifth inning. C.J. Russo contributed the key hit, a double to the left field corner. Hampton Bay's left fielder booted the ball into the woods and Russo advanced to third base as Ray DiMartino scored.

That's when the umpires huddled. The third-base umpire ruled the hit a ground-rule double, but was overruled by the home-plate umpire, who permitted DiMartino's run and ordered Russo to third base. Russo scored on a groundout by Phillips, before Mike Corelli's single scored Sean McGuigan.

This was a game with odd plays. The only damaging hit by Hampton Bays was a strange two-run home run in the third inning. A line drive was hit between Lepore and Russo on the right side of the infield that took a football-like bound past right fielder McGuigan.

There would be one more key play that saved Phillips' gutsy performance and the regional title. It was a pickoff in the sixth inning.

"Brian Lepore saw that the runner was way off the bag," said catcher Scott Minchak. "We have a signal between us. I was just hoping for a good pitch. The pitch before was wild."

Years later, Lepore said he thought the pickoff was one of the most important plays in Ardsley baseball history as he explained what happened.

"Bases loaded and we're playing in Mahopac with a chance to go to the regional finals," he said. "When there was a man on first base and there was a runner ahead of him, I wouldn't hold the runner on first base close to the bag.

"After the pitch was thrown and the runner would advance towards second base, Scott and I would tap our legs towards our hip with our fingers. Either I called it or he called it with that little hand signal. Then after the pitch was thrown I would get in behind the runner and the ball would already be on its way. It was a timed play."

This game and many others during the '86 season added to George Phillips' reputation as a pitching workhorse. George appeared in 25 of the 36 post-season innings the Panthers had played up until then. He had pitched in each of Ardsley's last five games, including three seven-inning stints. The big right-hander also saw action in each of the last three days, pitching a total of 11 innings.

"I'm just doing it for the team," Phillips told the *Gannett Westchester Newspapers* after the game. "I know I'm not going to pitch in college. I'm a hitter. I enjoy hitting. Right now, I don't care how much I throw as long as it benefits the team."

Phillips' performance against Hampton Bays was gutsy. He felt he had three-quarters of his normal speed on his fastball.

"I was trying to work on spots," said Phillips. "My arm was killing me yesterday. I was trying to move my fastball around."

"He hung in so tough," said Coach Fitzpatrick. "I can count at least 10 instances where I said I was going to take him out."

In the seventh and last inning it was all about George's determination. Hampton Bays' batters came to the plate looking for walks. There weren't any. What they found were George's strikes. Hampton Bays batters took only three swings that inning. Two of those three swings were good for strike three. The third was a pop-up to third.

After the game, Coach Fitz admitted that Phillips needed a little rest. But the next day after advancing to the state Final Four in Little Falls, New York Fitz began to wonder about his pitching staff. In all likelihood Phillips would be unavailable for a Saturday Eastern region matchup against Newark Valley of the Binghamton area. Coach Fitz could have called on the well-rested John Feinauer who was 6-0, or Chris Presbyto, 5-0. Could or would Fitz go to Phillips again?

Just before making the trip upstate, the '86 All-Section Baseball Team was announced. Phillips, Chris Presbyto, and C.J. Russo were selected.

"Going up to the state championship I didn't know what to expect," Fitzpatrick said. "But I had been around baseball a lot. I think the pep talk I gave before we left helped. I told them, 'look, I played a lot of baseball. We're good. Let's not count ourselves out. I am not lying to you guys. We're good.'

"Looking back now I could say that honestly because I played with guys who went to the major leagues like Mike Jorgensen of the New York Mets. I gave the team an honest evaluation. I felt very good about that."

Little Falls, New York, or more precisely, Ilion, now awaited Ardsley. The time gap between Ardsley's next game was important. Coach Fitz felt his boys minds were dialed in to the mystique of a state tournament rather than baseball itself. With some extra time he hoped they would think only about baseball.

The bus ride up state was a trip the boys would never forget. For Phillips the trip to Little Falls was the furthest upstate he had ever been as he gazed out the bus window to watch cows grazing.

Brian Lepore remembers the tiny bus that took the team upstate that year. "There was a small sendoff with few parents there. The next year there was a big bus and a great sendoff.

We were really nervous going up there. You are playing on a pro field. There was no talking.

"That was the big difference between the '86 and '87 teams. A lot of guys in '87 were fooling around in the bus. With the '86 guys there wasn't much talking. It was business. Everyone was good friends but it wasn't a goofball atmosphere.

"I was surprised that the bus made it to the high school to pick us up in '86. On the way back home the bus broke down close to Cooperstown. It was hot. We were tired. Coach Fitz wanted to take us to Cooperstown. But we were out partying the night before. All we wanted to do was go home. We didn't want to go to Cooperstown.

"We were all outside the bus and Fitz and the bus driver are underneath the hood looking at it. All my teammates were hunched over looking. All of a sudden Bernie McNerney is behind the steering wheel and beeping the horn. It scared the dickens out of everybody. Bernie was laughing his pants off. That made everybody feel happier. Eventually we jumped back on the bus. When we get together now we talk about that story."

Earlier, upon arriving in Little Falls the Ardsley boys got off the bus to revel in the surroundings at the ball field. What they also saw was a helicopter hovering above the diamond in an effort to help the grass dry from a day of rain.

"I didn't think I was going to pitch," Phillips said years later. "I thought John was going to pitch the first game. At this point we were just happy to be there. We had never been there before.

"We had a little conference and knew that last year the team that we beat made it to the finals and lost by one run. We thought we were better than them. When we took batting practice, their whole team sat in the dugout with their mouths open. They were intimidated right from the start.

"So Fitz comes up to me in the dugout before game one in the state semi-finals against Newark Valley and their pitcher Doug Whitmarsh and says, 'George, John's really nervous. Do you think you can go out there and just get me the first inning?'

"I go whew, my arms dead. Do you really want me to do that? Fitz goes, 'I need you to give me one inning and maybe John will calm down and he'll come in.'"

Phillips then went down to the bullpen area and threw to his catcher Scott Minchak.

"Some days you feel like the ball feels like a feather and it flies out of your hand," Phillips said. "Other days it feels like a shot put. That was one of those days when I felt I was barely reaching Scott. Scott, how does it look? He told me that I was throwing as hard as normal."

That's when the match between two great teams, Ardsley High School and Newark Valley, was about to take place.

13. BY GEORGE HE DID IT

There are times in everyone's life that are burnt into our memories. For the fifteen Ardsley ballplayers, one was the first time they stepped onto Murnane Field in Little Falls, New York, the site of the final four of the '86 state baseball championship.

Murnane Field harbors a lot of history. It was home to minor league baseball's Utica Blue Jays in the late '70s and early '80s, and then the Blue Sox. In 1983, the Blue Sox won the New York-Penn championship that was chronicled in the book, "Good Enough to Dream," by Roger Kahn, who owned the team that year. In 2002, baseball Hall of Famer Cal Ripken bought the team and moved it to Maryland.

On Saturday, June 13, 1986 Ardsley hoped to play two games at Murnane. If they won a morning contest against Newark Valley then there would be an afternoon game for the New York state Class C title.

Going into the tournament every team knew that Ardsley was a hitting machine. The stats proved that. But that Saturday morning in the State East Region final Ardsley's hitting would be tested. The Panthers would be facing Doug Whitmarsh, a 19-year-old right hander, who dominated Binghamton region baseball in '86.

Newark Valley was 17-3. Whitmarsh started 15 of those games and was undefeated. He also finished every game that he started.

Just like Ardsley's George Phillips, Whitmarsh was a workhorse. They both pitched at a time when there weren't any limitations on how many innings a pitcher could hurl. Whitmarsh pitched 19 innings between Monday and Tuesday, including Newark Valley's 12-inning 5-3 win over Section 6's Buffalo City in a Southwest Region final.

Whitmarsh might have been good but even he never faced a hitting team like Ardsley. That's also when Coach Fitz had made his decision. He would call on George Phillips and his tired arm one more time.

So it was Ardsley versus Newark Valley. It was a high school pitching duel everyone wanted to see, Phillips versus Whitmarsh. Ardsley fans had read about Whitmarsh's exploits. They wondered how tough he would be and whether Phillips could do it one more time.

George was up for the task. He threw a four-hit shutout at Newark Valley in Ardsley's 7-0 win that advanced the Panthers to the state final. That effort brought Phillips' total innings pitched in post-season play to 32. George's four-hit shutout was the first by an Ardsley pitcher that season.

Phillips threw seven good innings. He got the job done by relying on fast balls, curves, a split-finger change and a great deal of help from his teammates. He walked five batters, struck out seven while stranding eight base runners, even escaping bases loaded problems in the first and sixth innings. It was a gutty performance.

To end the first inning, he and second baseman C.J. Russo picked off a runner at second. Newark Valley even tried a suicide squeeze play in the fifth inning. George came flying in, scooped up the ball, and tossed it Scott Minchak who made a nice play blocking the plate.

Ardsley had many heroes. In the bottom of the third, Sean McGuigan was safe on a two-out error and then stole second. He scored on Chris Presbyto's single to left. Two innings later, Phillips walked with the bases loaded for an important second run. Then Ray DiMartino, the No. 9 batter for Ardsley, tripled with the bases loaded to ice the win.

More incredible about the game was the fact that Saturday's semifinal victory was Ardsley's fifth straight tournament win without an error. That was simply amazing. A good defense for sure wins games. A loose defense doesn't. Newark Valley was guilty of four errors.

Nearly everyone contributed to Ardsley's win. That was to Coach Fitz's liking.

"It's always been that way," Minchak told the *Gannett Westchester Newspapers* after the game. "If the top of the order isn't hitting, the bottom is. If the pitcher is struggling like George was, the fielding helps out. Hit the ball to us and we'll make the plays. Pitch to us and someone will hit the ball."

"The key was getting the off speed stuff over so the hitters didn't know what to expect," Phillips said in that same interview. "It feels incredible but we won't be satisfied until we have the championship trophy."

Throughout the game, a distinguished-looking, balding gentleman sat in the bleachers wearing bright green slacks. He wore those bright green slacks for the last five tournament games. George Phillips, a lawyer by profession, knew what a good luck charm can do. Certainly, the state semifinal baseball game wasn't the time to change trousers in the tournament.

George's father had quietly fought his own battle with nerves. His son, George, provided all the assistance the green slacks needed as Ardsley advanced to the Class C championship.

14. HEARTFELT WIN EARNS STATE TITLE

The straight news was that Ardsley captured its first Class C New York State baseball title in Utica in 1986 by defeating Adirondack Central 6-5.

As the years pass, that's what most people remember. But for the team, its coach, and Ardsley fans who followed the club all year long, there was another story, this one a heartfelt baseball story.

Whether it's a team rallying from a near-impossible deficit to win a game or a player coming out of nowhere to be great, these are the stories people remember.

Many in the crowd that Saturday afternoon of June 14 couldn't believe what was happening. Ardsley needed a starting pitcher for that championship game. George Phillips had pitched his heart out in previous games and couldn't go again. Coach Fitz could have called on Chris Presbyto or maybe Scott Minchak. He called on neither.

Instead, Coach Fitz went to his big right hander John Feinauer in the most important game in the school's history. Could John do the job? There were doubters because Coach Fitz had set him down for a two week stretch during the season. He didn't pitch in any sectional or regional games.

Earlier in its only loss of the season to Pelham High School Ardsley staked Feinauer to a six run lead. After that game John found himself sitting on the bench. As good a pitcher as he was, John was wild. He had a penchant for giving up lots of walks. That's not what the team needed in the season's last and most important game.

"The thing with John was that when he was on he was hard to hit," said George Phillips. "He didn't get hit around a lot."

"Starting Feinauer after a season of much wildness, I don't remember it being that dramatic," said Coach Fitz more than thirty years after the game. "I don't remember it being heroic starting him in that game. I don't want to give myself credit for doing something that really wasn't extra special. He definitely was struggling but he was a dedicated guy.

"He'd run around the track before every home game. He could throw the ball. It was just a matter of let's give it a shot. If it doesn't work out, we could have found someone else. He came through. That's one of the nice things about coaching when you make a decision and it works."

Pitching for the first time in nearly a month, John hurled a 7-hitter and walked just two batters. He slammed the Adirondack Central door shut by retiring six of seven batters after Ardsley took its final lead in the fifth inning. It was Feinauer's seventh win of the season without a loss. He was named the game's Most Valuable Player.

Neil Fitzpatrick had gambled on getting one more good game out of the senior John Feinauer, and the big guy hurled a classic game.

"I feel like I'm standing on top of the world," Feinauer told the *Gannett Westchester Newspapers* after the game. "I've had more strikeouts but I've never faced so much pressure."

When Feinauer walked off the mound, he'd thrown seven commanding innings. Probably at some time he thought that this was the last game he would pitch in high school.

"He showed me the kind of person he really is," shortstop Billy Bakker said in the same interview. "He's really had a hard time of it. We almost gave up on him, but he showed us he could do it when it counted."

Years later, Bakker said, "John could have pouted and just mailed it in and said I'm not pitching. He took Coach Fitz's benching in stride. He understood that he wasn't getting the job done. For a sixteen year old kid to have that attitude is just wonderful."

Feinauer's teammate C.J. Russo recalls another side of John. "I remember during pre-season stuff before we could get out to the field, John was 6' 6" and I was 5' 6". Coach Fitz would put us through all sorts of conditioning drills and I was Feinauer's partner. I had to carry him up the steps and he had to carry me up the steps. There was something unbalanced about that.

"John didn't have a position in the field but Fitz was determined. John found his niche in pitching. He had some struggles but he stuck with it and delivered some big game performances for Ardsley."

In this his biggest game against Adirondack Central, Feinauer gave up infield hits in the fifth inning, but the Panthers scored four runs in the bottom of the inning.

"We started most of the hitters with the curve and it screwed a lot of them up," said catcher Scott Minchak. "This game, everything came together for him in warm-ups. I know if we won the first game that morning, he'd get by."

Ardsley's bats came alive with two out in the fifth when Phillips tied the game with a two run triple, sandwiched by run scoring singles by Chris Presbyto and Mike Corelli.

"We've been that way all year," said first baseman Brian Lepore in a *Gannett Westchester Newspaper* interview. "Coach Fitz has been saying all year, 'Do it with two.'"

Early in the game the bottom of Fitzpatrick's batting order did the job as it had done many times when the upper half was stopped. Ardsley's Bakker bunted for a hit and Lepore and Minchak each singled to the opposite field in the second inning. The Panthers tied the game. Earlier Adirondack scored two runs on Minchak's throwing error in the first inning. Ardsley was stymied initially by Adirondack's left-hander Barry Hall who was staked to a 5-2 lead as his curveball threaded the inside of the plate. Then a right-handed relief pitcher came in to face George Phillips in the fifth inning. George was looking for a curveball. This time it was a hanging curve that he drove to the right field wall for a three-run triple that tied the game. Mike Corelli followed with a single to score Phillips with the winning run.

Many years after Ardsley's win, Coach Fitzpatrick had thoughts about his coaching career.

"You would think that the happiest moment of my coaching career were the four consecutive titles but it's not that simple," he said.

"Certainly, when Mike Corelli camped under the fly ball for the third out of the '86 championship it was surreal. My biggest memory is the last out for that championship. It was a fly ball. When the ball left the bat it was hit hard enough that I had no idea if it was a home run or whatever.

"But when I saw Mike waving his arm and saying, 'I got it,' it was truly the pinnacle. When the ball hit the glove I couldn't believe it. I just wanted to be a high school coach. This was incredible.

"Growing up I was never a champion. We had played against tough schools like Malloy. When Mike caught the ball it was unbelievable. The first one. It was very special. It never happened before. It was kind of like when you're a kid you read about these things happening to people."

The night Ardsley won the title for the first time Fitzpatrick said he was ecstatic but he didn't have somebody to share that joy with. Neil went to his brother Brian's house who was living with his wife Pat upstairs in his mother's home in College Point. Years later Coach Fitz would face the worst day of his life when he found out that Brian had taken his own life.

"The warmth and love I felt in their presence was a wonderful way to celebrate the best day in my life at least career-wise and vocationally," he said. "When you witness success of an athletic team, you notice that the smiles and glee can't be replicated.

"That first title was such a powerful thing that the following year I had to make sure that I didn't use that experience. We won the second and third. But the first was special. To be honest, when it was the fourth championship it was stressful for me. I didn't love it. It was self imposed stress. I was kind of waiting for the streak to be over."

On several occasions through the years Coach Fitz spoke about another aspect of that first championship game win.

"During warm-ups I recall how many coaches would yell at their players," he said. "Maybe I'm the sensitive sort, but I don't think I would have played as well for a coach who was embarrassing his players in front of the opposing coach and team.

"One of my favorite memories is from that championship game. As we were doing our infield practice, our third baseman Ray

DiMartino threw the ball to our catcher. It was so high, hard and wild that it would have gone into the dugout.

"I was hitting fungoes at the time. I reached out with my bare left hand and snared the ball and pretended that nothing had happened. I then hit another grounder. I did it so smoothly that I'm not sure anybody noticed anything out of the ordinary. That is what I wanted to go on. I was kind of proud of my practices that made us look good."

George Phillips maybe said it best about his teammates after they won Ardsley's first New York State baseball title. "We looked like a college team out there."

For many older Ardsley fans who watched the team perform all season long they probably recalled the New York Yankees of old when a popular saying was, "Rooting for the Yankees is like rooting for U.S. Steel". That's how good Ardsley was, U.S. Steel like.

The first five hitters in Fitzpatrick's lineup, C.J. Russo, Sean McGuigan, Chris Presbyto, George Phillips, and Mike Corelli each hit over .400 for the season. Russo hit .506 and stole 15 bases. Phillips hit 10 home runs and drove in 44 runs, in addition to compiling an 11-1 record and pitching four of the last five games. He pitched 32 of Ardsley's 57 post-season innings.

The rewards and acclaim followed. The school finished 24th in *The USA Today's* top high school baseball team rating compiled by *Collegiate Baseball.* Ardsley received an additional award by being named the No. 1 small school in the final rankings by the New York State Sports Writers Association.

When people in the New York metropolitan area picked up their *Daily News* paper on Sunday, June 29, news of Ardsley's success greeted them through a five-column headline, *Russo + Ardsley = No.1.*

Ardsley finished No. 4 in '84 when it compiled an 18-6 record, No. 2 in '85 when it went 22-2 and No. 1 in '86 going 26-1. That 66-9 record over those three years tells a lot about the growing dynasty Fitzpatrick was putting together. Those numbers for '86 included a per-game run total of more than 12, a team batting average above .380 and a batting order in which every starter hit over .320. The lineup was productive from top to bottom, with Russo topping the

.500 mark.

Yet despite the tremendous offensive production, Fitzpatrick said it was his team's efficient defense that was most responsible for the Panthers' big year. Ardsley's defense played a great part in their 26-1 season record. In the two pivotal games in Utica, the team committed just one error.

After the season's final win the Village of Ardsley pulled out all stops with a traditional motorcade parade on Saturday, June 21, 1986. Beginning at the Ardsley Middle School on Ashford Avenue, 10 cars headed toward the village business district on Saw Mill River Road. From there, the motorcade proceeded along Heatherdell Road to McDowell Park.

The sun was shining as people lined the streets and cheered all the players in uniform who were sitting atop the convertibles as the motorcade passed through the village's business district. Over 150 fans attended ceremonies at McDowell Park at the conclusion of the 10-car motorcade.

Local politicians, school and Little League officials gathered on the field at McDowell Park, where most of the Panthers' players first played organized ball. A banner reading "This is where it all began" hung from one of the dugouts.

"It seems like it's more important now," infielder Ray DiMartino said to the *Greenburgh Enquirer*. "It really made us think and realize what we did. It seemed so far away, after we won there was nothing else to do. Today I know what happened."

C.J. Russo, who started that decisive game winning rally, accepted a jibe from Little League representative Gene O'Gull, who said, "We gave you second base when you were 13; you never gave it back."

"This makes us feel like champions," Fitzpatrick said following the ceremonies. "We forget sometimes how many people we touch. We made people proud and it's hard to remember that other people had a hand in this too. This will be remembered by everybody, not just a few."

15. What Being a State Champion Means

All 15 members of Ardsley High School's championship team were asked by a *Gannett Westchester Newspapers* columnist to give their feelings about being part of the 1986 state championship team.

Had you been in Utica, you would have seen the jubilant pile of humanity at the pitcher's mound after the final out. You would have seen the glazed looks of young men who couldn't quite believe they were the best in New York State.

Luigi Assente – "Being state champs is the greatest feeling in the world. In my opinion, it's just as good as being World Series champions."

Billy Bakker – "Of course I'm excited about winning the states, but in a way I'm sad because I'm leaving a bunch of guys that were like brothers to me. I'm on a team that had a combined record of 76-4 in three years together. Twenty years from now, we'll all get together and remember this event and feel proud. I'm honored to be part of this special team. I'll never forget June 14 for the rest of my life."

Michael Corelli – "I guess the best word to describe the way I feel is satisfied. I'm not overly excited because we were the best team there and we should have won. I would have been very disappointed if we didn't win. It's a great way to end my high school baseball career. I was happy that all the hours we put into practice paid off. I think once I start to read about it in the papers, I'll start to realize how big a deal it really is."

Ray DiMartino – "This championship was a once in a lifetime victory. The significance of just one game was incredible. It's something to remember for the Village of Ardsley."

John Feinauer – "I think that winning the state championship is the most satisfying way to end a season. I am a senior and I'm going to be leaving high school. I feel that I am lucky to be a participant in a once in a lifetime chance."

Brian Lepore – "Being state champs is incredible. It is something that I will never forget. All the hard work finally paid off. We've reached our ultimate goal. We deserve it, and we are the best."

Sean McGuigan – "I will remember this championship season for the rest of my life. Being state champs is something very special and I will be able to look back on this accomplishment. It was a great way to end my senior year. My teammates were like another family. We were very close."

Chris McNerney – "Although I don't start, I'm privileged to be on such a solid ball club. I'm only a junior and I will be in the starting rotation next year. Next year, we'll be just as solid."

Scott Minchak – "The instant we won, it must have been the greatest feeling I have ever experienced. I cried. I was just so happy to know that we were the best in all New York State."

Noburo Ohrui – "All those tough practices we'd gone through made us state champs and I think we definitely deserved it."

George Phillips – "Winning the states was like eating a pizza with sausage and peppers...very satisfying."

Chris Presbyto – "Being state champions is a great feeling. We came close last year and going into this year we knew we had the potential. We worked hard in practice and it's a great way to end my senior year. I'll always remember it."

Cy Richardson – "Being state champions is the best feeling in the world. I really can't believe that we did it, but I think all those practices paid off for us and we earned it. We're the best!"

C.J. Russo – "This moment means the world to me. It's the extraordinary ending to a championship season. It's something to remember for the rest of my life. I won't forget this season or the great teammates I had."

Marc Scuder – "I was very excited about winning the states. I hope to see Little Falls and Utica next year."

A.H.S. Baseball Champs 1986 — Bottom Row: (Left to Right) S. Minchak, C.J. Russo, C. Richardson, L. Assante, N. Chrui. Middle Row: B. Bakker, C. Presbyto, R. DiMartino, M. Scuder, M. Corelli. Top Row: G. Phillips, C. McNerney, S. McGuigan, B. Lepore, J. Feinauer, Coach N. Fitzpatrick.

Billy Bakker 1986 shortstop on deck.

Shortstop Billy Bakker throwing to first base.

Brian Lepore sliding in 1986 Valhalla game.

Chris Presbyto

George Phillips.

George Phillips in 1986 was 11-1 and pitched 32 of Ardsley's 57 post-season innings.

George Phillips hits 10 homers to lead team in 1986.

C.J. Russo hit .506 and stole 15 bases in 1986.

"It's not just what C.J. Russo can do on a baseball technically, it's what he brings to the field: hustle, 150 percent effort, knowing how to win."

Season ending player motorcade becomes annual event.

1987

16. HOPES FOR '87

The spring of 1987 dawned and the nation's business cycle expansion extended through its fifth year. On the world scene, the U.S.S. Stark was hit by two Iraqi air-to-surface missiles killing 37 sailors. During a visit to Berlin, Germany, President Ronald Reagan challenged Soviet Premier Mikhail Gorbachev to tear down the Berlin Wall.

In Ardsley, Coach Neil Fitzpatrick was trying to create an attitude among his players that his 1987 team's success shouldn't have anything to do with the '86 team's state championship. He went so far as not to all any of his players to wear clothing emblazoned with 'Ardsley State Champs'.

"I told them that that was last year," he said. "I was pretty adamant that this year was brand new. Don't talk about that we were state champs last year. Let's see what we can do this year. I gave 100 percent not to put any undue pressure on them. I wanted each season to be an event in and of itself. Freddy Calaicone, a very solid first baseman from our early eighties teams, came back in '87 to help me coach. I know he admired that style."

What might be one of Fitzpatrick's proudest moments as a varsity coach occurred when Freddy was coaching the junior varsity and his team was doing ok but one parent got a hold of the superintendent's ear and complained about Freddy. That had to do with playing time for the parent's son. The parent wanted Freddy fired.

"When the parent, superintendent, and I had a pow-wow I made it clear that if Freddy left I would resign immediately," Fitzpatrick said.

My superintendent backed Freddy and me. Case closed. If you are not willing to go to the mat for assistants and colleagues you're not much of a coach."

The graduation of six starters, John Feinauer, George Phillips, Chris Presbyto, Billy Bakker, Sean McGuigan, and Mike Corelli led many to think that Ardsley would be rebuilding. But baseball is a pitcher's game, a popular phrase known to fans everywhere. And Ardsley had quite a few hurlers entering the '87 season, Ray DiMartino, Scott Minchak, a sophomore Bernie McNerney, juniors Mike Ferraguzzi and Brian Summer.

"I don't know who the ace is yet," Coach Fitzpatrick told the *White Plains Reporter Dispatch* at the time. "I don't have anybody I can describe as an overpowering pitcher, just guys who can get the job done."

Coach Fitz would eventually find and ride his pitching horse just as he did a year earlier. In '86 it was George Phillips. In '87 he would ride Scott Minchak. And for the two years after that it would be Bernie McNerney.

Three of four infielders returned, including All-Section second baseman C.J. Russo. Before the season opener Coach Fitz went so far as to call Russo the best baseball player in Westchester who could do it all, noting that he was fast, played good defense, hit, and hit with power.

Russo had a new partner in the middle of the diamond, junior shortstop Jeff Caldara. The other starting infielders, first baseman Brian Lepore and third baseman DiMartino, were back from '86.

The Panthers, strong up the middle, also had returning catcher and senior Cy Richardson, a former utility player who would blossom as an outfielder. The only uncertainties were two outfield positions and at third base when DiMartino was pitching.

Interestingly, Coach Fitz did something he had never done before. While he brought up a few sophomores, he now brought up a freshman, Tommy Caldara.

"Fitz, like every great coach, was looking to the future and he found it in Tommy," said Tommy's brother Jeff Caldara. "With C.J. Russo graduating in '87, Coach Fitz would have his heir apparent in

Tommy and boy did he see that correctly. Coach Fitz coached two of the best second basemen in Westchester County for such a long period of time."

Having played with both Russo and his brother Tommy, Jeff knew from where he spoke.

"They were similar," Caldara said. "Tommy and C.J. were the hardest workers on any of the teams that they were on during those championship runs. They were hard-nosed ballplayers. They took every pitch like it was the last pitch. Defensively they both had strong arms and good range.

"C.J. wasn't the biggest guy. He and Tommy both had power from the leadoff spot. They both could throw relief innings. They were the leaders by example. If they needed to, they were the guys who knew when to say, 'Hey Johnny, you better do this.'

"It was hard to differentiate between the two. Tommy was a little bigger. They both could throw from all arm angles. They could go get a ball in center or down the right field line as well as anybody. They could get taken out at second base and still turn a double play. They would get up and almost spit on the guy who was trying to take them out. They were cut from exactly the same cloth."

Jeff Caldara laughed when he spoke about playing with C.J. when Russo was a senior and he was a junior.

"I was almost more afraid of him than of Coach Fitz if I didn't do the correct thing, not that C.J. would yell at me. He would give me a look or an eye and say, 'You better get going here.' Tommy was unquestionably the same."

Mike Ferraguzzi, who also played with both Russo and Tommy Caldara, remembers them well.

"Both had great range in the field," Ferraguzzi said. "C.J. hit with more power. But when Tommy became a senior he had a very quick bat. Tommy would get up and he would get on base. C.J. would get up and look at the first pitch and maybe hit a triple or a home run out of the park. We were playing in the Irvington tournament and all the Irvington fans were screaming. C.J. hits the first pitch to centerfield halfway up a tree. We went to States in our junior year and on the first pitch of the championship game, C.J. hits a triple. He ends up hitting a home run after that.

"We didn't lose much with Tommy except a little power. Both were incredibly intelligent baseball players."

There's no doubt that the '86 and '87 teams were different. The '86 team was all business. So was the '87 club but they achieved success in a different way.

The '87 team was loose, fun, and full of humor with Jeff Caldara leading the way. As the teams evolved, Coach Fitz adapted to each one.

"When I was a senior, we could mess around with Fitz," Caldara said. "We could have conversations knowing that he would hear them. I remember when we were in the field taking batting practice, and Mike Ferraguzzi would say, 'Tommy' and we would chime in with 'Jen, Jen'. That was the girl Tommy was dating at the time.

"We would have this little banter. Years later, Fitz would say how much he loved that. That brought a different feeling. He grew with the kids. In the beginning it was all business. I remember when he was throwing BP and we would always throw the balls around the mound so that they would be easier to collect. A lot of times, I would try and throw a ball, and one hop it, trying to hit the protective screen. A lot of times I would hit him in the back of the leg. Fitz wouldn't say anything. He got it. He knew it."

17. THEY WEREN'T STRANGERS

Baseball was their first love. Well before they were teenagers they were playing with other Ardsley nine year olds in Little League. They surely weren't strangers to each other when they took to the baseball diamond in pursuit of a second New York State Class C baseball championship in 1987.

Who were these young Panthers? Each was unique in his own way.

One of the interesting things about Ardsley's baseball success in '86 and '87 was Coach Fitz's mixing of seniors like C.J. Russo and underclassmen like Frank Moretti.

On their 1986 state championship team, Russo, Brian Lepore, Scott Minchak, Ray DiMartino, Cy Richardson, Marc Scuder and Chris McNerney were juniors. In '87 they were the veterans who helped show the way to a new group of underclassmen.

Matt Arone, Jeff Caldara, Brad Chenard, Mike Ferraguzzi, and Brian Summer were the new crop of juniors and sophomores picking up the championship title baton.

C.J. Russo was the intense and clutch playing second baseman. Teammates were even afraid of him. Russo made you play better because you didn't want to disappoint him. There was no one who worked harder than C.J. When his teammates got nervous in the field, they would just look at C.J. for confidence. If there was a situation where a hit was needed who would they turn to, C.J. Russo, of course. He led the team in batting in '87 with a .492 average.

Neil Fitzpatrick said that Charles Joseph (C.J.) Russo might have been the best athlete Ardsley ever had. Nicknamed Roose, he was a pure, obsessive, born competitor who learned how to play baseball with his father Charlie in the backyard of their Yonkers home. That's where he started playing Little League ball before moving to Ardsley. His will to win propelled Ardsley to its first two championships.

He was named Westchester All-Section. As a leadoff hitter in '87, Russo led the Panthers with a .492 regular season batting average. He was the Class C Most Valuable Player of the state tournament, had 30 RBI, nine triples, three home runs, and was 16-for-17 in stolen base attempts.

Jeff Caldara played shortstop. Coach Fitz said that if he could pick one person, Caldara was his best captain ever. He was quite an athlete. Jeff played on both the '87 and '88 championship teams. Nicknamed Caldo, he was a jokester but in a great way. When it came time to play Jeff was always there. He along with other Ardsley football players like Ray DiMartino, Brad Chenard, Frank Moretti and C.J. Russo brought a tough football mentality to baseball.

Caldara had an outstanding arm, throwing the ball hard and effortlessly. The balls he did throw in the dirt weren't difficult to pick up because they were thrown so hard that they took nice bounces. It seemed everything in sports came easy to him. He batted .358 in 1987.

Jeff stepped in for Billy Bakker in '87 after Billy graduated. It was like Didi Gregorius following Derek Jeter at shortstop for the New York Yankees. Like Didi, Jeff had big shoes to fill. There was no way Jeff was going to let down for a second and be a second class shortstop. He filled the void. Besides being an outstanding athlete, he carried Ardsley's winning tradition further on the sidelines as its baseball coach for several decades.

Coach Fitz liked to tell this story about Jeff. When Ardsley went back to Little Falls in 1987, Fitz's friend Ed Miles, who Neil described as an Ardsley biology teacher extraordinaire and undefeated freshman football coach, went up ahead of time to make sure everything like hotel arrangements and meals were set up for the players.

"I felt that in 1988 Jeff Caldara took over that role," Coach Fitz said. "It is not that he had to make room accommodations or anything like that, but he made sure that all of the equipment was transferred properly, that the players took their duties seriously, that practices were zip-zip, and that everybody was on task. That was an amazing performance. I could not have asked for an assistant coach to do as well. In '86 Billy Bakker performed much of the same role."

Cy Richardson played left field. According to Coach Fitz, Richardson went as far athletically in college as any of Ardsley's alumni. He was recruited to play in the Atlantic Athletic Conference (ACC). He had accepted a scholarship offer to attend the University of Maryland but at the last minute enrolled at the University of North Carolina where there was a slot for a walk-on player. His first two years at UNC Cy found himself playing the outfield. The last two he played the infield and was captain of the team. He batted .333 in his senior year.

Richardson's baseball career came a long way. It showed his perseverance. In his junior year at Ardsley, he held the scoring book and mostly sat on the bench. He was in a Class C high school somewhere in New York state holding the book. In his senior year, he was in left field. His practice paid off. In '87, he made some of the best defensive plays on the team. He had a rifle arm from the outfield. He batted .380 that year.

Cy's first baseman Brian Lepore remembers when he took cutoff throws from Richardson, Cy would always throw the ball at his head that almost hit him like a bullet. Cy was a competitor who never chirped to anyone. He just did his business. Lepore said that Richardson and Frank Moretti, another Ardsley outfielder, got the best bead on the ball off the bat. Their first step was always the right step.

A great teammate, Richardson had an affable personality and got along with everybody. When he took the field there was nothing but a big smile on his face.

Ray DiMartino held down third base. In previous years, he found himself near the bottom of Ardsley's batting order. But in '87 he was usually in the fourth spot. He had blossomed. He was a character, a jokester. Nicknamed Demo, he kept his teammates loose. You could always hear some laughter coming from DiMartino and Jeff Caldara on the left side of the infield.

Ray was kind of aloof. When game time came, he didn't look like the most natural guy, but time after time he would come up with big hits. A talented athlete, DiMartino made things look easy. He had great hand-eye coordination and came up with one of the biggest catches of the '87 season against Eastchester High School.

As a senior, DiMartino was named an All-Section player. He led Ardsley with 37 RBI and batted .419 during the regular season. In eight post-season games, DiMartino went 14-for-27 and led the Panthers with a .519 post-season batting average.

Brian Lepore was back at first base in his '87 senior year. He tried to model his game after Keith Hernandez of the New York Mets. Throughout his career, Brian saved many errant throws from his Ardsley infielders.

Brian and Jeff Caldara would go at it back and forth. To this day, Brian still tells youngsters who Caldara coaches at Ardsley that he (Lepore) saved their coach so many errors because he picked so many balls out of the ground. Lepore had soft hands, was a great teammate, a clutch performer who may have struck out twice his entire high school senior season.

Brad Chenard in right field was another player who took his football mentality to the baseball field. A hard worker, he has been described as a quiet assassin. Anytime he stepped on the field, whether he was playing right field, first base, or just walked into the batter's box, you knew you could depend on him. He batted .358.

All Brad wanted to do was win. That had nothing to do with personal accolades. In the outfield, he had a strong arm. He was rather shy. He was just business. He wasn't a chirper. He stayed to himself and let others do the talking. He was incredibly humble and religious.

When he was in the batter's box, he was often called "the human rain delay". After almost every pitch Brad would leave the batter's box, readjust his gloves and helmet, step into the box and take 10 seconds more. By then, he was ready to hit the ball.

Matt Arone was behind the plate. His teammates nicknamed him the puppet because when he ran he was kind of lanky and every appendage seemed to go in a different direction. He looked like a puppet or a marionette. That didn't keep him from calling a good game for Ardsley's outstanding pitching staff. He knew where to locate the pitch and his work ethic was second to none.

Matt spoke positively and as a catcher was very vocal. He knew the game well and was an integral part of the most famous defensive play in Ardsley's long baseball heritage that took place in that '87 season.

Frank Moretti patrolled center field. He was quiet and shy. His personality was different than many of his teammates. He didn't have that sense of humor that most had where they could rib each other. Frank would get a little perturbed when someone would bust his chops and everyone would hear his little cackle if he was abused. That doesn't diminish the important role Frank played on this championship team.

He made not just great catches all season long. He made big catches. He was a sparkplug who had speed, could steal bases, and had the quickest jump on a fly ball hit to the outfield.

"I remember how diligently he worked during batting practice, perhaps too much," said Coach Fitz. "I tried to tell him that he didn't need that much. He wouldn't give. He kept working because he wasn't happy with his offensive performance."

Frank's teammate Brian Lepore recalls how all the parents would be at home games. Pat and Lou Ferraguzzi, Bart Caldara were among the regulars there.

"You would see this little old man with white hair sitting alone in centerfield by the bleachers," Lepore said. "He also would lean against the fence. I used to hear him say whenever I would be up at bat, 'Come on Brian, hit a good one. Nice swing Brian.'" That was Frank's father.

There are times when some athletes rise to the occasion on a grand stage. Frank saved his best for last. The 5-foot-7, 130-pound centerfielder was one of the offensive and defensive stars in the '87 Class C baseball tournament semifinal and final victories. He was the straw that stirred the Panthers attack. His defensive plays in both games saved Ardsley's season.

Scott Minchak made the transformation from primarily catching in '86 to becoming one of Ardsley's premiere pitchers in '87. He earned All-Section honors with a 9-0 record and an ERA below 1.00. The right hander's best outing came when he pitched 6 2/3 innings of perfect ball in defeating Pelham High School.

Some teammates remember calling Scott "Farm Boy" because he liked landscaping. On occasion, Scott could be found raking the baseball diamond. On the mound in '87, he threw countless innings and gave up very few walks. While he didn't overpower anybody, he just hit his spots. Also nicknamed "Mini", Minchak always threw strikes even though he had a funny sidearm pitching motion. He had what might be called a swerve, a slow sidearm pitch that baffled batters. He even threw that way when he was catching. Scott could throw every day if needed.

How good a pitcher was **Bernie McNerney**? Coach Neil Fitzpatrick said Bernie was the best pitcher he ever coached. That says it all.

Bernie got called up to the varsity at the end of his sophomore year. He made a deal with Coach Fitz. Bernie wanted to be able to hit. He didn't fair too well. His nickname for that '86 year was "O for varsity". However, it didn't take long for McNerney to dominate on the mound. As he got stronger and stronger as a sophomore he pitched a couple of big games. He was just becoming a great pitcher.

McNerney, a sophomore starting in a state championship game (1986), threw lights out. He was a competitor, a talented, talented pitcher. He just wasn't scared. There was no fear in his eyes. He didn't care and showed no emotion. He just laughed and worked.

His teammates knew Bernie was a character. When he was pitching his infielders were afraid of him. When he was having problems on the mound he wasn't afraid to tell his teammates to get out of his face because he had the situation well in hand.

For a fellow who was tall and lanky he didn't have the greatest athletic body. He was just a tremendous athlete, an All Section basketball, baseball and football player.

He had the naturalness that you cannot teach. While he wasn't a great hitter he came to grips with that. His teammates still rip him about it. He knew his bread and butter was what he did on the mound. He was one of those players you couldn't teach what he could do. He did everything so well. When he pitched he worked a mile a minute. As a defender, his infielders loved that. He threw strikes.

An outstanding teammate of Bernie called him a gamer who took football to the baseball field. Throughout his high school career he threw endless innings. He pitched quite hard and could overpower some opponents. He would mix up his pitches. He was smart and truly liked pitching. Bernie enjoyed the process, not just throwing the ball. His teammates always knew he was going to give them big games.

Brian Summer was classic in the way he mixed up his pitches. He wasn't going to overpower you. He was going to throw a great curveball. He had the best curve of all the pitchers on the team along with the best fundamental windup. He was a low key guy who you knew when he took the mound was going to throw strikes.

Brian was crafty and smart beyond his years as a pitcher. As a freshman, sophomore, junior and senior, it has been reported that Brian never lost a high school game while he was pitching. His record might have been 22-0.

With Summer pitching, opponents were going to put the ball in play and Brian's infielders had to play defense. They remember that every time they made a good play in the field, Brian would take his glove and just point it at them.

Brian was mellow, laughed a great deal and never got angry. If you made an error behind him, he would just look at you, slap that same glove and say, "It's all good. Let's get the next play."

Summer was called "Marty" by his teammates because that was his father's name. His dad was well known in Ardsley's Little League.

Brian got everything out of his talent. He might have thrown just 78 or 79 miles per hour. His pinpoint control went along with a nice curve ball that kept batters off balance. He knew he had a good defense behind him.

Teammates still joke about the time Brian and some teammates went to a Ponderosa Restaurant at the state championships. Mike

Ferraguzzi was on line at the buffet table and passed gas. Brian looked at Mike. Brian, a proper type of fellow, looked and said, "Michael, that's not how you are supposed to act in a restaurant." Brian was dead serious. The teammates laughed but everyone got the message.

Mike Ferraguzzi had no equal as a relief pitcher. Coach Fitz said he was like former Boston Red Sox pitcher Dick Radatz. "Mike would just come in and mow people down," he said. "The thing I remember about Mike is that he worked out tremendously. In our pre-season gym workouts I couldn't believe how many sit ups he did. Those strength workouts helped him. He came in and just threw flames."

Mike was a cut-up and could give it back as well as he took it. He might have been one of the most intelligent players on the team. He got everything out of his talent. He fluctuated with his weight and as he moved up in high school class he knew he had to handle it. Mike didn't have the fastest hands but he knew how to hit a baseball.

However, he found his niche as Ardsley's greatest closer. Mike's relief pitching contributed greatly to Ardsley winning the state title in '87 and '88. He was on the mound at the end of both games when Ardsley won the state championships. Mike's role was unique in high school baseball. When a pitcher tires, high school coaches usually brought in the shortstop, catcher or centerfielder to pitch. These are players who were already in the game.

Mike Ferraguzzi was different. He was a specialist. He was a closer. That was his primary role. In C ball, that is unusual. The fact that Ardsley had a specialized closer, who actually warmed up on the sidelines, was unheard of.

He was cool as a cucumber on the mound. Mike also played a lot of right field as a junior and senior and had a strong arm. But as a designated hitter and closer, that's where Mike was at his best.

18. OH THOSE BURMERS

With the temperature in the fifties on Wednesday, April 8, Ardsley opened its new a new '87 baseball season in a new league.

Now playing in League 7 against the likes of Eastchester, Pelham, and Pearl River there were no breathers in the schedule. In fact, the team lost four early season games and found out that they weren't unbeatable by any means.

In the season opener Ardsley pounded out 15 hits in beating Byram Hills, 14-7. Ray DiMartino went 3-for-5, including a two-run home run. Ardsley's formula for success throughout the season was on display in the win as Mike Ferraguzzi got the victory, pitching the last 3 2/3 innings in relief of starter Brian Summer.

Two days later, Byram Hills handed Ardsley its first defeat of the season, 4-1. Ardsley then played in the Irvington Hudson River Tournament and leadoff hitter C.J. Russo picked up from where he left off in the '86 season. He went 5-for-5 including three RBI and had three stolen bases as the Panthers beat Nanuet 18-4. Again Ferraguzzi came on in relief and picked up his second win of the season.

Ardsley fans got a chance to watch Brian Summer win his first varsity decision in the River Tournament. One teammate, Russo, was already a successful senior, the other, Summer, a hopeful junior. They had more in common than their Ardsley uniforms. They and many of their teammates played on a junior varsity squad that had won 51 consecutive games. Its last loss came in 1984. All-Section second baseman Russo was a freshman on the JV team which began the streak. He only played one year at that level but recognized how important it was to the varsity's success.

"With the JV winning all of those games, it's gotten the varsity into the right frame of mind," Russo said in a *White Plains Reporter Dispatch* story. "We've always had a lot of hop in the infield and the outfield, and we've always had a lot of hustle, which Coach Neil Fitzpatrick likes. There were also a lot of little things I learned on the JV, things like backing up your teammates, and being a team player." By this time in the '87 season Russo was 13-for-16 at the plate and batting .813. Meanwhile Summer, who had just picked up his first varsity win, played two undefeated seasons on the JV.

"During our freshman year, Coach Brian Connolly taught us hitting, base running, pickoff moves, and especially how to play as a team," Summer said in that same interview.

Many years later, Coach Fitzpatrick would sing the praises of Connolly who went on to have an outstanding football coaching career at Edgemont High School. "He strove for excellence and was very determined to be good. I never had to give him any kind of advice. He knew what he was doing and put in a lot of effort. The players really respected him.

"My philosophy was to stay away from JV and freshman baseball. I thought it was none of my business because I had done a lot of freshman and JV coaching and I didn't want the varsity coach Bill Graney telling me what to do."

Mike Ferraguzzi remembers Connelly as being very much like Coach Fitz. Both believed physical mistakes were no problem whatsoever but mental mistakes were not to be tolerated.

"Connelly was definitely more intense than Fitz," Ferraguzzi said. "We ran so much for Connelly. In practice if you made a mental error that would be a burmer. Everyone ran together after we lined up at home plate one after another. We would sprint to first, jog to second, third and home. Then we would sprint home to second base and jog all the way home. Then sprint home to third and jog home.

"Just like in the military if one person messes up the whole team was going to run. Obviously no one wanted to mess up and make their teammates run. We actually once won a game but we didn't win in the fashion that we should have. So right after the game we ran while the opposition was looking at the team wondering what was going on."

The three mental lapses Connelly didn't like were getting a ball hit to you and not knowing where to throw it; two teammates calling for a ball and the ball falls between them; and not hitting the cutoff man on a throw.

So there were few mental mistakes early in the '87 season as Ardsley's bats remained hot. The 4-1 Panthers knocked off Bronxville 14-4. On the mound, Ferraguzzi struck out nine en route to a complete game victory. Ardsley won three of its first four games in a big way putting together a plentiful supply of extra base hits in wins over Byram Hills, 14-7, Nanuet 18-4, and Irvington 16-1.

Besides Russo's phenomenal start to the season, center fielder Cy Richardson was batting .357. Third baseman Ray DiMartino, batting third, had seven RBI. Cleanup hitter Brian Lepore was batting .333 and also had seven RBI. Catcher Scott Minchak was hitting .286. Shortstop Jeff Caldara was tied for second in batting at .357. Junior Mike Ferraguzzi had compiled a 3-0 record and another junior Brian Summer was 2-0 in the early season going.

Ardsley was soon 6-1. Then however, the Panther bats and pitching faltered and two more losses followed. One was to Rye High School. As the team was packing up and getting ready to get on the bus for the ride back to Ardsley, Coach Fitz saw Cy Richardson's father, Gerard, sauntering in from the right field stands where he was quietly watching the game. Fitz was expecting some comforting words like, "Don't worry boys, we'll get them next time."

Instead, Gerard said, "So now you know how it feels to lose. It's time for you and your lads to get off your high horses. You've been winning too much." Mr. Richardson was from England, taught English at Fox Lane High School in Bedford, NY, and took his sportsmanship seriously.

Richardson's words must have had an impact. Ardsley wouldn't lose another game for the rest of the season. The streak started with a 6-1 win on May 1 against Pearl River. Winning pitcher Scott Minchak tossed a five hitter to lead visiting Ardsley, 8-3 at the time, to this league victory. Brian Lepore had a two run triple in the first inning as Ardsley picked up three quick runs. Meanwhile, Mike Ferraguzzi was tied for the third most wins in the county with a 4-0 record.

Six days later, Minchak finished with a two hitter after hurling perfect ball for 6 1/3 innings in a 6-1 win against Pelham. Ardsley broke the game open in the third when Ray DiMartino smacked a two-run homer to left center.

Ardsley pitching history was soon made when sophomore Bernie McNerney won his first varsity game for the host Panthers. He beat Pearl River 18-3. Everyone seemed to get into the act. Russo went 4-for-5 with three RBI. Lepore had four RBI. Brad Chenard went 4-for-4 with two RBI. Frank Moretti went 3-for-5 with one RBI, and Jeff Caldara went 4-for-4. Ardsley improved to 10-4, 7-3 in League 7 play.

Then for the second game in a row Ardsley's Minchak had a shutout bid spoiled, this time by a seventh inning homer. The right hander finished with 10 strikeouts and one walk in a 9-1 win over Edgemont High School. Amazingly, it was the only walk he gave up in his last two starts covering 14 innings.

Edgemont had a rematch three days later and the result was even more lopsided. Ardsley won 13-2 and Brian Summer improved his record to 3-0.

Meanwhile, by then no one in Westchester was pitching with as much control as the Panthers Scott Minchak. This time in Ardsley's 10-0 win over Westlake Minchak threw five innings of shutout ball before leaving. Scott was now 5-0 and in five starts gave up just three walks and three runs, relying mainly on a fastball and sharp breaking curve. In this outing against Westlake Scott didn't walk anybody. He struck out two, and limited the losers to three hits.

The folks in Ardsley were becoming increasingly interested in the Panthers and began wondering whether the team could take another state title. They were now in the Section 1 Tournament.

19. Minchak Stingy with Walks

Bill Fischer shouldn't mean much unless you're a real baseball nerd. He was a journeyman pitcher for most of his major league career. But in 1960 he did something that has never been duplicated.

On August 3, he walked Cleveland third baseman Bubba Phillips leading off the bottom of the first inning. He didn't walk another batter until the last game of the season. His pitched 84 1/3 consecutive innings without allowing a walk, still a major league record.

Ardsley's Scott Minchak wasn't Bill Fischer in '87, but he might have had dreams about that record as he left the mound an Ardsley winner in a Section I quarterfinals game on May 28. Ardsley beat Dover 19-0. For his fourth consecutive outing, Minchak did not walk a batter. In the fifth inning he had a 3-0 count on a batter but everyone on Ardsley's bench knew he wasn't going to give up a walk.

With that win Minchak improved to 6-0 while only issuing three walks for the season. In that outing he got a lot of help from his friends. Every starter had at least one hit. Cy Richardson and Brian Lepore had four hits apiece to lead the Panthers, the tournament's third-seed.

The win got Ardsley a game against second seeded Valhalla in Class C's semi-final that Ardsley won 12-4. Richardson's grand slam in the fifth inning and Minchak's two run homer in the third were enough for Ardsley. Both shots cleared the left field fence. Ray DiMartino went 3-for-4 for the Panthers, and C.J. Russo went 2-for-3 with a walk and three runs scored. He had a double and triple.

Young Bernie McNerney picked up the win and his record went to 2-1.

Coach Fitzpatrick was delighted with the center field play of Frank Moretti who saved two runs for Ardsley in the home second that preserved a 2-1 Panthers lead. Later, Russo retreated from his second base position to rob the Vikings of a pair of bloop singles in the sixth, and Richardson dove to catch a short fly to left in the seventh.

The win sent the 15-4 Ardsley Panthers to Rye Neck for the opener of the best of three Class C finals. By then Ardsley was scoring in double digits in almost every game. In this Class C opener, Ardsley won 13-5 as DiMartino went 3-for-4 and drove in five runs. Winning pitcher Brian Summer allowed just one run in six innings. The junior right-hander kept Rye Neck baffled with a big curveball and sneaky fastball. He struck out two, walked two and allowed just one run after facing a no-out bases loaded situation in the fourth.

Against Rye Neck it didn't take long for Ardsley to get going. The Panthers took an early lead, scoring three runs in the first on an error, a single by Richardson, a two-run triple to right center field by DiMartino and an RBI single by Brian Lepore. Ardsley piled it on with six in the fourth inning. Three straight Ardsley batters walked to load the bases. Richardson hit a sac fly to center for one run, and DiMartino, Lepore, Chenard, Scott Minchak and Caldara hit consecutive singles to drive in five runs. Lepore finished 3-for-5 while Richardson, Brad Chenard and Jeff Caldara each had two hits.

Ardsley couldn't wait for its next game. A few days later, Ardsley won its third straight Section 1 Class C championship with a 10-1 win over Rye Neck to sweep the best of three series. The Panthers pounded Rye Neck pitchers for 17 hits. Ardsley's win was a showcase for the team's top three hitters, Russo, Richardson, and DiMartino. The trio accounted for six runs, ten hits and five RBI. It was the eleventh game in a row that the Panthers scored in double figures, a far cry from earlier in the season when they lost a couple of games possibly because they thought they could coast.

On the mound winning pitcher Scott Minchak just needed a two-run first inning for the victory, his seventh without any losses. Amazingly he issued but three walks and four runs in his seven starts, while his teammates scored 64 runs. Minchak knew he had to go seven innings in the heat against Rye Neck so he paced himself from the start and just followed his basic philosophy of throwing strikes. That was quite a change in roles for Minchak who was the '86 team's catcher. In '87 he became the team's mainstay pitcher.

At the game was Fred Calaicone, the Pace University baseball coach, and the fellow Russo would be playing for in the years ahead.

"I've watched C.J. since he was a 12-year-old little leaguer," Calaicone told the *White Plains Reporter Dispatch*. "It's not just what he can do on a baseball field technically, it's what he brings to the field: hustle, 150 percent effort, knowing how to win."

Now it was on to Brewster and another sectional meeting with Marlboro High School, a team Ardsley knew quite well.

20. CALDARA'S HOMER KEEPS SEASON ALIVE

One of the great parts of baseball is the fact that a game can be decided with one swing of the bat in the last inning. In baseball parlance it's called a walk-off home run that ends the game. Thus the losing team (the visiting team) must "walk off" the field immediately afterward, rather than finishing the inning.

There have been a lot of iconic home runs in Ardsley's long baseball history. None may have been as important as junior shortstop Jeff Caldara's dramatic bottom of the seventh lead-off blast that lifted Ardsley to a 6-5 victory over Marlboro High School in the Section 1 Regional Class C game at Brewster. The home run kept alive Ardsley's dream of defending its state baseball title.

It was a moment that remains seared in Caldara's memory. He remembers the overcast day at the Brewster field when he was the first Panther to come to the plate in the bottom of the seventh. As he walked up to bat he knew he was 0-4 and had struck out a couple of times. He wasn't thinking about hitting a home run but he knew he had to contribute something to help the team.

Once he was in the batter's box Jeff remembered what Coach Fitz had always said, "You could be 0-4 but as long as you are contributing in the field and thinking positively, good things can happen."

The first pitch from Marlboro relief pitcher Al Angelone was a ball. The next was a strike. Determined to give himself a chance,

Caldara swung at the next pitch, a curveball, something he was looking for. He met the ball square on and sent it flying to left centerfield. Ardsley players on the bench jumped to their feet. Their eyes were glued on the ball. Everyone had the similar thought: That ball had a chance of leaving the ballpark. It kept climbing. The ball cleared the fence, some 340 feet from home plate.

After the game Jeff told the *White Plains Reporter Dispatch*, "It's unbelievable, great, anything you want to call it. I started running to first, and then I just took my time around the bases. I wanted to savor the moment."

"The exhilaration and excitement, I didn't understand it as I was running around the bases," Caldara said thirty years later. "I saw all the guys come to home plate. As I rounded third base I got absolutely mauled.

"The way I can describe it best is talk about my dad who was not the most affectionate guy. As soon as I was mobbed, I started heading to the dugout. The fans in the stands are going crazy. My dad comes and grabs me and gives me the biggest kiss on my cheek, and says, 'You're awesome. I love you.' I had never really heard that until his dying days."

That was Caldara's first home run of the season, and he admitted that it was his first major hit since a Little League homer that won a championship game.

To begin the game, Coach Fitzpatrick turned to sophomore Bernie McNerney as his starting pitcher. McNerney, 3-1, had trouble in four of the seven innings but hung in as he labored to get the victory. He gave up nine hits but escaped by stranding eight Marlboro runners on base. Even though he struggled Bernie seemed to get better as the game went on.

Ardsley had tied the score in the third without benefit of a hit. Ray DiMartino walked, went to third on two groundouts and scored on a wild pitch. Then in the fourth inning Ardsley scored four times. Scott Minchak's double and Frank Moretti's single started the comeback. Two walks, three stolen bases, an error and Brad Chenard's two-run single finished the scoring.

But Marlboro wasn't done, scoring twice in the fifth and adding a run in the sixth to close the gap to 5-4. In the seventh Marlboro tied the game. Enter Jeff Caldara, stage right. Ardsley was now moving on to a Class C State quarterfinal game against Valley Stream North at Eisenhower Park in East Meadow, Long Island.

21. TRIPLE PLAY FOR THE AGES

They still call it the play. They also still call it amazing. You had to be there to see and believe what happened. A lot of parents who missed it said, "Thank God I wasn't there. I would have had a heart attack. There's no way I would have survived."

It's hard to imagine any single Ardsley fielding play ever creating as much excitement and lasting discussion as what happened on June 3, 1987 at Eisenhower Park on Long Island. Ardsley was the beneficiary of a triple play to end all triple plays. Many fans say it's still the most important fielding play in Ardsley baseball's history. If you saw what happened you probably wouldn't disagree.

Ardsley came within one inch of ending its season instead of traveling hundreds of miles north to Little Falls and the New York State Class C Championship Final Four.

That inch separated Ardsley catcher Matt Arone's glove, Valley Stream North runner's outstretched hand, and the successful continuation of a crazy triple play. That all took place in the game's last regular inning, the seventh, of Ardsley's 11-7, nine-inning win at the Southeast Regional Final.

The play was all the inspiration the Panthers needed. Ardsley's four runs in the ninth sealed the victory. Earlier however the Panthers first had to pull winning pitcher Scott Minchak out of huge trouble in the seventh. Valley Stream North had tied the game 7-7. Now Minchak faced a no-out, second-and-third situation. Ardsley's bus driver probably had his keys in the ignition and was ready to head home.

Minchak looked at Valley Stream's Ronnie Lundgren. Instead of walking him to set up a force out at any base, Minchak got him to bounce to a pulled-in Ray DiMartino at third. DiMartino gave a quick glance over at John Salerno taking his lead from third base. That glance was enough to hold him there. Ray threw to first for the out. Salerno broke for home and first baseman Brian Lepore threw a strike to Arone. Arone's lunging sweep caught the diving Salerno's fingertips by an inch and saved Ardsley's season.

But the play wasn't over yet. Arone came up throwing to shortstop Jeff Caldara who was now covering third base. Caldara put the tag on the sliding Valley Stream runner for the final out.

"It happened so quick, I didn't want to tag him without the ball," Arone told the *White Plains Reporter Dispatch* after the game. "The ump said later I got him by an inch, it was that close."

Fitzpatrick was still amazed when the game ended.

"I've seen great plays, but second and third, no outs, a base hit away from winning and you get a triple play? That's unheard of."

The triple play sent the game into extra innings. It gave Ardsley the boost it needed after blowing an early 7-2 lead. Minchak's seventh-inning walk was his first in five starts. He was laboring and had given up four runs and seven hits over the last three innings of regulation. Fitzpatrick however stuck with Scott. Valley Stream's Lundgren meanwhile pitched seven innings in relief.

Ardsley finally figured Lundgren out. A slow curve hit Brad Chenard. Jeff Caldara's single sent him to second. Mike Ferraguzzi moved the runners with a sacrifice, and Frank Moretti drove in a run with a single to left. C.J. Russo followed with an RBI single to center, Cy Richardson then hit the clincher, a two-run triple to deep left field.

What was it like on the baseball diamond in Eisenhower Park before and during this triple play? Coach Fitzpatrick and Ardsley's players have their own recollections three decades after it happened.

Ray DiMartino started the play at third base. He remembers listening to Coach Fitz when he came out to the mound before the triple play pitch. He remembers how loose Fitz kept everyone in that moment.

"He (Coach Fitz) came out and talked to our pitcher and said, 'You know what, let's go get him out somehow. We're going to get a pop-up to the infield or we're going to get a come-backer to the pitcher's mound and we're going to get one out. Maybe then we'll walk a batter to keep the force for a double play. We're not going to worry about getting the second or third out. We're going to get the first out.'"

DiMartino recalled that once Ardsley turned the triple play and ran off the field everyone was going crazy. "I knew at that point the game was over and we were going to win somehow. That's what makes it so enjoyable. The fans remember you. I bump into people and they still talk about the triple play all these years later. Some even remember it better than I do."

Brian Lepore said the triple play was ridiculous. "I remember looking over at C.J. and thinking that we lost the game. "Then we didn't. The throw to me was coming from third and I saw the runner break immediately for home. I knew there was no time. I threw a pea to Matt Arone and it was in the perfect spot. I'll never forget that throw. We had practiced that throw."

Cy Richardson was playing left field and admits that it didn't dawn on him that Ardsley needed a triple play to get out of the inning.

"It was a ground ball to Ray at third. I came in from left to back up the play. After the third out was made I came in and asked Brad Chenard whether Ardsley had won. I was jumping up and down. Brad told me no, that we were going to extra innings. I didn't know what was going on there was such bedlam after that play."

There was one person in Ardsley's dugout who was saddled with making the decision of what to do. That was Coach Neil Fitzpatrick.

"If you follow high school baseball, the most important factor in not losing games is to put the ball in play," Coach Fitz said. "Invariably, a base runner who gets a free pass scores while the guy who gets on because of an error gets doubled up. I have no science to back that up. But I know Yogi Berra would have understood that.

"And if you ask somebody with some baseball savvy what do in this predicament, he probably would say walk the next hitter and now you'll have a force out at every base and a better chance to stay in the game. Not only that, but we had Scott Minchak on the mound so he was not going to walk in the winning run.

"But that was nagging at me when a couple of players sidled up to me to suggest that we take the traditional approach and walk the next batter to load the bases so we would have a force out at every base. I decided not to walk the hitter because another walk would lose the game.

"The play at home was so close that I would not have made a peep if the umpire had signaled safe. But the call was out and that was our second out. The runner on second base was watching the action at the plate ready for the safe signal so that he could jump in the air in celebration of the regional championship. With his late start to third base, our captain and shortstop Jeff Caldara was already at third base waiting for Matt's perfect peg to catch that runner sliding into the base for out number three.

"If we didn't win the state championship this second year I seriously doubt that we would have ever gone back to Little Falls. Never mind winning it four years in a row."

There are other back stories to that incredible play. Tommy Ferraguzzi, who was the catcher on Ardsley's '89 team, was in the stands at Eisenhower Park watching his brother play. His parents had him run down with quarters to call the Little League field at McDowell Park in Ardsley to let them know what was happening on Long Island. He was giving play-by-play descriptions to the snack bar at the Little League field.

Before the game, Chris Gordon and Mark Szafran got into Ardsley High School's band room and borrowed some musical instruments. They showed up in the game's parking lot along with Joe Pagano and began playing the horns and banging the drums. That started the madness and insanity that was part of the game's atmosphere.

Ardsley had but a day or two to savor that winning feeling before boarding a bus to Herkimer, New York to meet Albany area's Watervleit High School in the state semifinal. Watervliet, 26-6, had won its third consecutive sectional crown in '87 and was the '85 State Champions.

For the young Ardsley ballplayers, it was an exciting time at 8:30 in the morning when the high school did the right thing as the boys got ready to leave for the championship games. Walking out of the high school's front door they found a receiving line waiting for them as they made their way down the 15-foot wide concrete path towards the bus. A majority of the 600 classmates and many teachers lined the walkway patting them on the back and offering good luck wishes.

They climbed up into the bus now decorated in blue and gold bunting. Chants about Ardsley baseball and a constant drum beat cut through the air as the bus door closed before heading up state and a date with history. Once on the bus things settled down as the young players just became high school kids again. Then a great deal of attention turned to Bernie McNerney who was sick and continually coughed up phlegm. They realized how sick he was but would later marvel at the courage he would show on the mound.

"Just being up there at the semi and final games was something else," said C.J. Russo years after he played his final two games for the high school. "You just couldn't grasp the whole experience. I remember when we stepped on the field the amount of emotion you had.

"When we got off the bus up there it was like, all right, here we are at a minor league stadium. This is the real deal. It reminded me a little bit like the movie *Hoosiers* when the players step into the basketball arena and hear that the hoop is only 10 feet high. The bases are only 90 feet apart. The pitcher's mound is 60-feet 6-inches away. Let's do what we always do."

That Friday night the team ate dinner at Bob's Big Grill, an Italian restaurant that received mixed reviews. They stayed at a local Days Inn where Coach Fitz paid particular attention to room assignments. A captain was assigned to each room and a senior as well. Sophomores brought up that spring were interspersed among them.

The following morning in Herkimer the Panthers received a five-hit pitching performance from Scott Minchak in beating Waterveliet 6-2 in the semifinal.

Little Frank Moretti, Ardsley's 5-foot 7, 130-pound Panther centerfielder had a career day that was part of his career weekend. He singled to start the four-run fourth inning and singled with two outs in the sixth to set the table for C.J. Russo's game clinching two-run homer in the win.

In the field, Moretti's catch of a deep fly to center in the fifth inning turned a potential game-tying hit into a sacrifice fly. An inning later, Moretti made a spectacular diving catch of a line drive. Ardsley now had one more game to play in a few hours, a championship match up against Western Regional winner Greene High School.

22. NEW YORK STATE CHAMPIONS AGAIN

C.J. Russo had to take it all in for a little while. Win or lose, he knew this was the last game of his high school career.

"The emotion overcomes you at first for a brief time," he said more than 30 years after that '87 championship game. "When I stepped up to the plate as the leadoff hitter I had chills."

It didn't take long for Russo to make his point just as he did in previous years. A senior, he played on three Section 1 championship teams and was an integral member of the 1986 state title squad.

Now in the '87 title game, Russo lashed the first pitch of the game for a triple.

"The emotional aspect of the whole thing was pretty overwhelming," he said. "But once you start playing the game, it's just a game again."

Russo's shot helped put Ardsley High School in front by eight runs in a 10-5 victory over Greene High in the New York State Class C Baseball Championship. The Panthers were up 4-0 five pitches after Russo's triple. By beating Greene, Western Regional winner, Ardsley became the first team to win consecutive state baseball crowns.

In that four-run first inning outburst by Ardsley, Cy Richardson followed Russo with a sacrifice fly to left. Ray DiMartino singled. Then Brian Lepore smashed the first pitch for a 400-foot homer to left center. Brad Chenard grounded out and then Jeff Caldara blasted a 2-1 pitch for a homer to left.

Frank Moretti led off the second with a walk. Russo homered to center, and the Panthers were at it again. They scored two more runs on two hits and three walks. Russo finished the day 4-for-7 with two homers, a triple and four RBIs. Earlier that morning in a semi-final game, Russo had walked twice and flied out to center before hitting a home run over the fence in right center field.

Now in this the season's last game, sophomore starter Bernie McNerney was plagued with a flu bug and his teammates quickly realized Bernie wasn't his usual self. He gave up five third-inning runs on five consecutive hits. Brian Summer came in and picked up the win. It was left to Mike Ferraguzzi in relief who finished up by getting the Panthers out of a bases-loaded jam with two strikeouts and a game-ending groundout to Russo.

No one was surprised about Ardsley's hitting assault as the Panthers compiled a sizzling .395 batting average for the '87 post season. Through the regular season it was .345, .362 overall for the year.

Russo set the pace batting .492 with 30 RBI, 9 triples, 3 home runs and 16-for-17 in stolen base attempts. Ray DiMartino led the team with 37 RBI while batting .419. Richardson hit .380, Ferraguzzi .367, Lepore .363, Caldara .358, Chenard .358, Moretti .276, Minchak .250. Minchak also finished with a 9-0 record to go along with a 1.00 ERA.

While the tournament committee selected Russo as MVP, and it was justified, there was quite a bit of sentiment for Moretti who was one of the offensive and the defensive heroes in the tournament's semifinal and final victories.

Frank singled to start the four-run fourth inning and singled with two outs in the sixth to set the table for C.J. Russo's game clinching two-run homer in the 6-2 semifinal victory over Watervliet. Defensively, he tracked down and caught a deep fly to center in Watervliet's fifth inning. An inning later, he made a spectacular diving catch of a liner to end that frame.

In the 10-5 championship win over Greene High, Moretti walked to start Ardsley's four-run second inning, walked, stole second and scored the ninth run in the fifth, and doubled in the last Panthers run in the sixth. Defensively in the championship game, Moretti raced back to the centerfield fence in the fifth inning, jumped a foot and a half and robbed a Greene's batter of a home run. A year earlier Moretti watched the Ardsley bus pull away for the state tournament without him.

Each Ardsley player had lasting memories about that championship weekend. Many reflect about taking it all in when they first stepped on to the Little Falls Veterans Memorial Park Stadium that is now the home of the Mohawk Valley DiamondDawgs of the Perfect Game Collegiate Baseball League. It was once the home of the Little Falls Mets where their heroes such as Dwight Gooden and Wally Backman once played.

Jeff Caldara called the Stadium the most pristine field he and his teammates had ever seen. "One of the umpires there told me that he had umpired at Shea Stadium and that this field was better," Caldara said. "After our team had infield and outfield practice there I didn't want to leave the field." Outfielders were shagging fly balls and Caldara, a shortstop, went out there to take extra fly balls because he didn't want to leave.

The win was a good cause to start celebrating. Today the players now readily admit that getting beer wasn't a problem in '87. Mike Ferraguzzi recalls how beer was in the Days Inn's bathroom along with a great deal of ice. "Two chaperones, Michael Burke and Dr. Hugh Kirshinsky, knocked on the door and said, 'Beer check.' They walked in, grabbed two beers and as they were walking out said, 'We were just checking to make sure it was cold gentlemen,'"

By the following morning it was time to go home. As they were leaving, the gravity of becoming the first team to repeat in the tournament's seven-year history wasn't lost on Russo.

"Repeating is the toughest thing to do," Russo said in interview with *The White Plains Reporter Dispatch*. "Nobody ever did that. It's just unbelievable. It hasn't sunk in yet."

Memories about that '87 championship season last forever and so do souvenirs from those upstate New York ball fields. A beautiful "Welcome to Murnane Field" wood sign somehow ended up in Jeff Caldara's backyard.

"We wanted a piece of the memory," said Cy Richardson who was Caldara's teammate. "We were in a dream state and we wanted to memorialize that." That was a time when Richardson and Caldara thought they were Captain America and called each other that for some reason. The two got into Murnane Field and the sign soon found its way on to the bus heading back to Ardsley. Richardson and Tom Caldara also hooked up to steal home plate from the Herkimer High School field.

The bus ride home was something each of their teammates would remember the rest of their lives. They roared, laughed and clapped. And then somewhere along way, they started singing. With a tape player blasting, the sound and voices cut through the bus. They knew the words to "We Are The Champions" ....We are the champions, my friends, And we'll keep on fighting 'til the end. We are the champions. We are the champions. No time for losers 'Cause we are the champions of the world. That would be there song for then and forevermore.

Finally their bus rolled into Ardsley, coming to a stop in front of the high school. The players peered out to see toilet paper rolls hanging from trees and classmates and adults sitting on the curb waiting to congratulate them. Beneath a red stop sign was another sign, Panther Mania.

Ardsley soon honored the team with a motorcade that took the team from Ardsley Middle School to the high school, past many residents who stood and cheered along Ashford Avenue. Sitting atop each open convertible adorned with blue and gold streamers were three players. Their destination was Ardsley's baseball field where bleachers were erected in front of home plate. Village, county and state officials spoke to nearly 200 adoring fans.

That's when Coach Fitz looked back on the year. "The one thing that's great about this team is a complete lack of jealousy," he told the *White Plains Reporter Dispatch*. "The players all feel good about being part of a team." He also thanked the players' parents for having shaped good character.

"You've got to have character, confidence and the players to win," said center fielder Frank Moretti. "Without the coach, we couldn't have done it. He threw batting practice every day. We miss batting practice already."

In that same story, Nancy Russo, the mother of Ardsley standout C.J. Russo, expressed the pride the community had for the team.

"Ardsley is a small community, and the parents are involved with their children; that's what brings us closer together," Russo said.

The highlight of the season for Fitz was watching his team develop into a squad capable of winning a second straight state crown. "It was a real pleasure because we had our ups and downs," he said. "We had our tough losses. We just got better. To watch them get hot through the tournament was just a pleasure."

Soon the awards started arriving, a second straight Class C championship for Ardsley earned the Panthers a second consecutive No. 1 rating in the *Daily News* annual post-season poll of Westchester baseball teams. Three players represented the champions on the All-Section team: Russo, Ray DiMartino, and Scott Minchak. All three would graduate. How would that affect the '88 team?

A.H.S. Baseball Champs 1987 — Bottom Row: (Left to Right) C. McNerney, G. Tarr, S. Minchak, C. J. Russo, R. DiMartino, B. Lepore. Middle Row: B. Summer, M. Ferraguzzi, J. Gruning, J. Caldara, B. Chenard, M. Arone, F. Moretti. Back Row: Ass't Coach F. Calaicone, M. Morel, S. Gyimesi, T. Caldara, B. McNerney, Coach N. Fitzpatrick.

C.J. Russo led Ardsley with .492 average in '87 and was named Class C MVP of the New York State tournament.

Frank Moretti offensive and defensive catalyst in Ardsley's '87 state tournament's semifinal and final wins.

Scott Minchak 9-0 record and 1.00 earned run average in '87.

Ray DiMartino led '87 team with 37 RBI while batting .419.

C.J. Russo, left, and Cy Richardson celebrate a win.

After big '87 state tournament victory.

Panther Mania awaits '87 team at high school.

Three players to a car at '87 celebration.

1988

23. WE DON'T REBUILD WE RELOAD

If there ever was year with a motto that embodied Ardsley's baseball team it surely was 1988.

Five key starting players graduated the year before, C.J. Russo, Cy Richardson, Ray DiMartino, Brian Lepore and Scott Minchak.

That surely should have dampened the Panthers' hopes for repeating again as Class C state champions. But someone in Ardsley read an article about a team from northern Maine that wore a shirt emblazoned with "We don't rebuild. We reload". That became the watchword for every Ardsley player in '88.

The reloading began when shortstop Jeff Caldara found a new second baseman to take the place of Russo. It was Jeff's brother Tom. Like Russo, Tom would go on to become the best second baseman in Westchester County. He started the season batting towards the back of the order. Three games into the season Coach Fitzpatrick changed that. Coach Fitz was loyal but if you weren't doing the job, he wouldn't take you out of the lineup, but rather he would move you around. That's what he did with Frank Moretti who moved to the back of the lineup.

Tom Caldara was now Ardsley's leadoff batter and he was only a sophomore. Besides playing second base, Tom also found himself appearing on the mound in a relief pitching roll. He along with his teammates Bernie McNerney and Steve Gyimesi would become the only Ardsley players ever to win three state titles. Caldara was the only one to take a trip to the states all four of his high school years.

Batting behind Caldara was another newcomer to the lineup, Steve

Gyimesi, who pitched and played right field. He was quite an athlete, lean but incredibly powerful. He had a quick bat. Coach Fitz once said that he thought Gyimesi was the most draftable player he had ever coached. Steve had all the tools. He was fast. He had power and was good defensively. When Gyimesi pitched McNerney played third, Craig Stephens sat and Mike Ferraguzzi played right field.

There was more to Steve. He was a light hearted guy who smiled and laughed a great deal. On the mound he was wilder than Bernie McNerney, Brian Summer and Mike Ferraguzzi. He walked a lot of batters but threw hard from a three-quarter angle that would tie other teams up and scare the heck out of them because of his wildness.

Another newcomer was Mike Morel, a junior who was an unassuming guy who played left field. He was unassuming because Ardsley had bigger talents on the team. Mike never spoke much but defensively there were few in Westchester high school ball who played left field as well as he did. It seemed every angle he took on a hit to left field was the right angle. It didn't matter if the ball was hit on the ground or in the air. At least three times during the season he made plays towards the left field line where he threw runners out at second base who were trying to stretch a single into a double. He knew the game and played it correctly.

Nicknamed "The Mayor" Morel had another side to him. Look out to the outfield sometimes and Morel would be tossing his glove up in the air. By the time the pitcher threw the ball Mike had his glove on.

There was more to Ardsley's reloading with Craig Stephens playing third base mainly when Bernie McNerney pitched. Craig had a great glove and coach Fitzpatrick actually said that he thought Craig, as a junior, if he was on another team would have been an All-Section player.

Returning senior seasons were Frank Moretti in centerfield, Jeff Caldara at shortstop, Matt Arone behind the plate and Brad Chenard at first base.

Caldara had all the tools. At the state tournament in '88 the most valuable player award could have gone to a bunch of players including Caldara. Defensively, he was outstanding, particularly going back to short left field to make catches. In an '88 playoff game,

Ardsley was winning 8-0 when the opposing coach came up to Coach Fitzpatrick and asked him, "Has this kid been playing like that all year?" Fitz replied, "Yes, he's definitely that good." There were three captains on the '88 team, Caldara, Moretti and Chenard. Jeff was definitely the unspoken leader.

Ardsley's '88 pitching staff was one of the best in the school's history featuring Bernie McNerney, Brian Summer, Steve Gyimesi, and Mike Ferraguzzi in relief. Coach Fitz would ride his ace Bernie McNerney in '88 and '89. Bernie and his pitching partners rarely walked anyone, a common theme for all four championship seasons. They all walked few batters, put the ball in play so that their teammates would make the right plays in the field.

"Bernie was the laziest athlete I ever met," said his lifelong friend Mike Ferraguzzi. "He never lifted weights and didn't like to run. His nickname was the "Vampire". He was strong as hell and a phenomenal athlete. I would never want to fight the guy. The nicest guy in the world but as tough as it gets.

"As pitchers we had to do a 12 minute run, Brian, Bernie, Gyimesi and me. Bernie and I would duck into the bathroom while Gyimesi and Summer were doing their laps. We would throw a little water on our faces and run back out to the track and finish the running.

"Bernie may have been lazy as all get out but put him on the mound and forget about it. At that level when you have a fastball like he had and a curveball, he was absolutely dominant. In a playoff game against Mattituck, I never saw anybody with that kind of control. It was like watching a surgeon."

Brian Summer holds the distinction of never losing a game he pitched in during his high school career. His record was 22-0. Nicknamed "Marty" because that was his father's name, Brian relied on pinpoint control and a nice curve. He didn't have a hard fastball at all. He just kept batters off balance. After a team faced Bernie and his fastball, they couldn't hit Brian.

Vinnie Fatato didn't play his junior year but made the team in '88. He was the fastest player on the club and was Ferraguzzi's official pinch runner.

In 1988 Ardsley had a unique advantage, the team had an official relief pitcher, something unheard of in high school baseball at that time. Mike Ferraguzzi picked up where he left off the year before. He threw extremely hard and pitched in relief for a few innings each time he was on the mound.

"Teams would be used to seeing the other pitchers," Ferraguzzi said. "I was most effective when I came in for Brian Summer because they saw his slow pitching and then had to face my fastball. I didn't throw junk, had no curve. I loved being a relief pitcher. People would say to me that it must be so nerve-racking. Actually it made me totally confident.

"Even coming into the game at States with the adrenalin flowing I probably had five extra miles per hour on my fastball. My issue was that if I wasn't a relief pitcher and had to pitch longer, my fastball by the fourth inning would have been flat and much slower. The fact that you could throw three starting pitchers out there and a designated relief pitcher, it was unheard of at that level."

Ferraguzzi readily admitted that closing out the last games of the '87 and '88 seasons to cinch the championships was the highlight of his high school career.

"My junior year I surprised myself. Senior year I didn't want Brian not to finish the championship game but I was actually thrilled that I got into the game and was absolutely juiced. Without a doubt winning those games in front of our parents was the best. Our parents had much more fun than we did. They were nervous as hell. They got to travel to see us play."

Each of Ardsley's players had a story to tell during that '88 championship season. One of them had a more dramatic narrative than any strikeout or home run. Eight months earlier Brad Chenard, the left handed hitting first baseman, was near death.

Chenard's story could have been the most tragic of any of his teammates. Brad was an all-section football player. He had to sit out the last game of the '87 football season against Byram Hills because he was sick. No one knew how sick he was. The left handed first baseman was near death.

"I suffered from spinal meningitis. I went into a coma for nearly two days. I was in critical condition," he told Maury Allen of the

White Plains Reporter Dispatch. All Ardsley players and cheerleaders had to take anti-bacterial medicine. While his parents prayed, Chenard rallied. He recovered rapidly, returned to school and hit .382 for the '88 season while on heavy medications.

There was one more person who Coach Fitzpatrick said elevated the team to a higher level in '88. It was Paul Murphy.

24. PAUL MURPHY ARDSLEY'S 'CRASH DAVIS'

When Paul Murphy, one of Ardsley's greatest athletes, returned to help the '88 team it was like a page out of a movie script.

Think of Clint Eastwood, a stranger riding out of the desert into an isolated mining town, in *High Plains Drifter.* Or better yet, think about the '88 American romantic comedy sports film *Bull Durham.* The film starred Kevin Costner as "Crash" Davis, a veteran catcher brought in to teach a rookie pitcher about the game in preparation for reaching the major leagues.

Paul Murphy was Ardsley's version of Clint Eastwood and "Crash" Davis. A Delaware resident and former third baseman in the Baltimore Orioles' system, today Paul is a Philadelphia Phillies area scout responsible for covering much of the Mid-Atlantic region, including Virginia. Earlier while playing at the University of Delaware he was named the 1986 ECC Conference Player of the Year.

Growing up Paul was all-section in baseball at Ardsley in the early 1980's. In 1983 Murphy became the fifth Ardsley athlete to win the Con Edison Athlete of the Week award. A year earlier *The Daily News* selected him as the best shortstop in Westchester. As a junior he was All County hitting .500 while striking out only once. He managed a still better campaign as a senior hitting .540.

I'll leave it to Jeff Caldara to set the stage about Murphy's '88 return five years after graduating from Ardsley.

"Growing up I used to go to Gould Park in Dobbs Ferry and watch Paul play American Legion ball with my brother John," Caldara said. "He was my idol. He was a shortstop like I was. He gave me one of his extra gloves. He was always good to me at that age.

"Now move forward to 1988. I will never forget it. The sun was going down. It was late March of our senior year. We had a very good winter so we were on the field early in the season. Our first game was a week away. It was a cold day maybe 50 degrees. We were practicing and all of a sudden I looked to my left at the bleachers behind the first base dugout. Paul Murphy is standing there.

"I looked at my brother Tommy and said, 'Tommy, that shouldn't be.' Murphy was supposed to be entering another season of pro ball. We had our practice and went to the locker room and saw Neil Fitzpatrick go over and have a conversation with Paul. The next day Neil tells us that we're going to have some help. Paul Murphy has volunteered to help us out.

"Later at practice, Neil came over to me and told me that Paul had been released from A ball in the minor leagues and that he was very dejected. Neil said that this is the way he wanted to get into baseball. Paul is a baseball lifer today. That was a God send. He brought us his baseball knowledge which was incredible.

"What Fitz couldn't offer in terms of basic mechanical stuff, Paul did not overlook. Paul would point things out. He wouldn't run up to you. He would provide adjustments.

"He helped me in making the double play. I'll never forget when I used to take the throw around the bag, if I got to the base early I would be impatient and I would come through and to receive the ball I'd be through the bag. A lot of times I would receive a bad throw and wouldn't be able to adjust left or right. Paul would tell me that I was there early and should slow play it. 'You're at the bag and this way you're going to get everything on your throw.'

"He was incredible. He was more incredible for the guys who didn't play. We had guys on our team who could have been starting for any team. They enjoyed his humor on the bench, his baseball isms. Here's an example. Somebody would hit a long home run off Bernie McNerney early in the season. Paul Murphy said, 'Throw a strike, get a bike,' meaning you throw a strike like that against a good player, you're going to need a bike to find the ball.

"Those little things were incredible in keeping the team loose and relaxed and that was on top of what he could provide for us. He missed two games our senior year because of job interviews. We lost both games."

Mike Ferraguzzi has his own thoughts about Paul Murphy. "Paul had all the lingo, all the quotes used by minor league baseball players." said Ferraguzzi. "Once I hit a line shot off of a Byram Hills pitcher. There wasn't a fence at the ballpark. Anybody else on the team would have had a home run, but I barely made it to third base. While I was rounding the bases, Murphy was yelling from the bench, 'Guzzi, keep making lefts. Keep making lefts.' The players on the bench were in stitches. Murphy looked at the players and said, 'Geez, he stops at all the deli's.'

"If Murphy saw a fellow on the team who wasn't playing much, he would ask Coach Fitz, 'Well, he's not a great hitter. Does he have wheels?' Paul's intent was to figure something out.

"Paul was an incredible assistant coach. He wouldn't step on Fitz's toes but Fitz obviously recognized that Murphy knew his baseball. Murphy never nitpicked and never tried to change a batter's stance. It was more about giving advice. He knew what was going to happen before the ball was hit. That was a big thing with Ardsley. When we were playing the field it was almost like we were running through everything in practice. We knew what to do with the ball before it came to us because we ran over that in our minds.

"We would say to ourselves, if a ball gets hit to me with a fast man on first base, I'm going to throw to second base and not to third base to try and throw him out. We knew we had to keep the batter who hit the ball on first base.

"When Fitz forgot something that's the only time Murphy would get in there. By the end of the '88 season he was Ardsley's assistant coach. The players also looked up to him because he was younger and had been through the baseball wars."

Tommy Caldara is one more player who remembers Paul Murphy's influence on the '88 team.

"Paul Murphy was larger than life," Caldara said. "He came back to our little team. It was baseball magic joining us. He would be there to fine tune us. He had the best one liners. He ate, drank and slept baseball. He would always have a big chew of tobacco in his mouth. He would tell you just the right things.

"He was so much fun. That was just another piece to the puzzle. Ok, we have this pro prospect here and he is working with us and rooting for us. That is another reason to get better today. He would tell stories and guys would crowd around. He would make us hysterical. He knew the game. He would walk up to the field and join in drills."

Looking back, Paul Murphy may have been Ardsley's most influential player ever.

"He's the whole story, really," Coach Fitzpatrick said in a 1983 *White Plains Reporter Dispatch* interview about Paul's high school play. "Murphy really set the tone. He brought the whole club to a higher level. Considering everything, I think he is the best ballplayer in the county. He just does everything."

Coach Fitz has always had soft spot in his heart for Murphy. In discussing Paul for this book, Coach Fitz said:

"Paul Murphy was not a speed demon. He wasn't really big. He wasn't really muscular. He was just a real good, solid baseball player. He did everything very well. He had a good attitude. He was on my first varsity team as a sophomore. I had him for my first three years of varsity coaching.

"He brought a level of professionalism. He was a great baseball player, not just good. He knew the game. I remember a phrase he used that kids on our '88 team probably laughed at. I had never heard it before. When a ball was hit that would become a home run, he would say, 'That dog can hunt.' That meant you could hit the ball a mile. When he came back to help in '88, he added tremendous things to that team. If I didn't have Paul Murphy as my first shortstop who knows what would have happened.

And then in true movie fashion after that '88 season, Paul Murphy rode out of town forever just like Clint Eastwood would do.

25. ALL IN THE FAMILY
JEFF & TOM CALDARA

What a good feeling it must have been when brothers Jeff and Tommy Caldara trotted out to their respective Ardsley High infield positions at shortstop and second base to start the '88 season.

Three-hundred fifty plus brother combinations have played Major League baseball. It's hard to find a shortstop-second base combination on that list. Through the years there probably haven't been more than a few if any in Westchester high school baseball. Jeff and Tommy were something else in the one year they played together.

Taking the field for Ardsley High wasn't the first time the brothers played ball together. When Jeff was twelve and Tommy was ten they were teammates in local tournaments as part of a club that a newspaper dubbed 'The Little Engine That Could.' The team knocked off teams from much larger White Plains, Mamaroneck and New Rochelle. The Little Engine was a team from a small village, Ardsley, that hung with anybody because the players were such a cohesive group.

Growing up at 33 Gould Avenue in Dobbs Ferry both boys were introduced to sports early on. That's where their father Bart was from, a three sport All County athlete in football, baseball and basketball. It was impossible for Tommy and Jeff not to pick up good habits from him.

Even when Bart was a Pop Warner football coach in Dobbs Ferry where all the Caldara brothers played, Tom had his baseball glove was with him so he could have catches at Gould Park. More catches took place in their backyard.

Both brothers were always competitive. "I think I showed a little more outward emotion which can work either for or against you," said Tom. "Jeff was always more in balance and neutral which is very important as a player and as a coach. He stays even keel which is important in baseball. I kind of wore emotion a little more on my sleeve. That's a blessing and a curse in a sport that is so mental like baseball."

Shortstop Jeff's best friend in the Ardsley infield was Tom. On the diamond they were in constant communication. Whether it's who is going to cover the bag on an attempted stolen base or who has the cut-off throw, they knew it was important that they were on the same page.

"Since we knew each other it was basically body language communication," said Jeff. "We didn't need to speak much to each other besides mouthing who has the steal. We were both so well versed in the game that we knew we would be in the proper spots."

Even today, Jeff talks to his own girls all the time about what a special moment he and their uncle Tommy had growing up as athletes in Ardsley. He also talks about how he was the luckiest guy in the world playing with the two best second basemen in the county, C.J. Russo and Tom.

The combination of brothers Jeff and Tom wasn't lost on their coach Neil Fitzpatrick.

"At the age of 28 I had my fill of softball so I decided to go looking for a baseball team to play on," said Fitzpatrick. "I ended up playing for a Whitestone, New York team and the following year my 19-year-old brother Brian joined it. This was such a blessing in my life.

"When Jeff and Tom performed as a double play combination in '88, I distinctly remember a picture of the two of them posing at second base. That was a photo to cherish."

There were more than a couple of poignant and funny moments when both brothers were on the field together. On April 5, 1988 the two played together for the first time in a 15-3 win over St. Raymond's. They both had two RBI.

Jeff laughed when he recalled hitting a home run in that game. "The best part of that game was the feeling our parents had." "That was what I always loved the most. Dad never missed a game. Our mom never missed a football game. Tom and I played on the same team in the fall.

"When baseball came around it was even more special. It was tremendous for me because you grow up with somebody you shared the same room with, you fought with every day, and you go through the same trials and tribulations. It was a special moment especially when you are those two people in the middle of the diamond and you both play such an integral role."

Tom Caldara remembers the first time he was called in as a relief pitcher on April 20, 1988 in a game against Rye High School.

"I hadn't pitched at any point," Tom said. "It was a close game, a big game. Coach Fitz came out from the dugout. He called the infield in to the pitcher's mound to talk. Then out of a complete surprise, Fitz turned to me and said, 'Tommy, you ready to pitch?' I said, 'Ok.'

"I was surprised. I had no choice because he was asking me. I got in there and was doing my warm ups and the other infielders backed off. My brother Jeff stayed and said, 'You better not screw this up.'

"I'll never forget. I pitched an inning or two and we got the win. Jeff's comment was just hysterical because Jeff was being a brother and you have that relationship. That was pressure but it was motivating too."

Fittingly, Jeff Caldara had a career year in his '88 senior season. He led the team with five home runs, 37 RBI and 39 runs scored. Along with Mike Ferraguzzi and Bernie McNerney he was named an All Section 1 team member. Brother Tommy's time would come the following two seasons.

26. RUNS RUNS AND MORE RUNS

The fall of 1987 crept closer to winter. In October, the world's stock markets crashed on "Black Monday" with the Dow Jones Industrial Average falling nearly 23 percent. The Minnesota Twins beat the St. Louis Cardinals in the World Series. In Ardsley that fall, the Panthers football team finished 3-5 and Dan Dantzic and Pam Rosen were named Homecoming King and Queen.

Soon the baseball team would be unlimbering arms indoors in anticipation for another run at the Class C state baseball title. On April 5 at home Ardsley opened its '88 season where it left off the year before with a convincing 15-3 drubbing of St. Raymond's. The Panthers were just getting started.

Bernie McNerney threw a complete game and had six strikeouts. Brad Chenard went 4-4. The other big news about that game was the fact that for the first time, Jeff and Tom Caldara played high school varsity baseball together and they shared the spotlight as well. They both had 2 RBIs.

Ardsley would soon score runs, runs, and more runs all season long at an alarming rate. By season's end Ardsley had 10 or more runs in 14 of their 28 victories.

Two days later, seven different Ardsley players drove in at least one run as the Panthers beat Bronxville 16-5 for its 15th consecutive win dating back to May 1 of the previous year.

The win came with a little anxiety built in. Ardsley fell behind 5-1 in the top half of the second inning. That deficit didn't last long as the Panthers scored five runs in their half of the inning. Mike Morel, who went 2-for-3 with three RBI, knocked in two of the Panthers runs. Matt Arone, 2-for-3, four RBI, and Tom Caldara each contributed an RBI to the second inning scoring. Frank Moretti went 2-for-3 and stole five bases. Brian Summer won his first game of the season and Vinny Fatato caught fly balls for the last three outs.

The Irvington Hudson River Tournament at Irvington's Memorial Field is an event Ardsley has owned through the years. This year was no different. Steve Gyimesi's bases-loaded single in the seventh inning gave Ardsley a 5-4 victory over Sleepy Hollow in the opening round.

Shortstop Jeff Caldara started the rally when he led off the seventh with a walk. Eventually Sleepy Hollow pitchers loaded the bases and Gyimesi ended the game with a single between shortstop and third. Mike Ferraguzzi won his first game of the new season.

In the championship game that followed, Bernie McNerney picked up the win in relief and drove in the game-winning RBI as Ardsley beat Nanuet 4-3. McNerney's double to center field in the sixth inning drove home Jeff Caldara from second base.

Mike Ferraguzzi remembers that game quite well. A Nyack player lined a shot to Caldara at shortstop. Jeff leaped and snagged the ball. It was a great play and all his teammates were applauding and hooting and hollering.

Ferraguzzi wanted to have some fun with Coach Fitz and said, "Hey Fitz, that looked like you in your prime." Fitz was offended and turned around and said, "I could jump higher than that. Murphy, tell him I could jump higher than that." Ferraguzzi quickly realized that was the last time he could try sarcasm in talking to his coach.

Now in game after game Ardsley prevailed. At Sleepy Hollow, Steve Gyimesi led the Panthers, going 3-for-4, including five RBI and a grand slam homer over the center field fence. That top of the fifth inning rally gave Ardsley the lead for good. Brian Summer picked up the win in tossing a seven-hitter.

Then in a rain-soaking win over Nyack with the temperature at 36 degrees, the Caldara brothers were at it again. This time Jeff and Tom combined for six hits and had three RBI each in a 18-4 win. Mike Ferraguzzi picked up the win going six innings. It was the Panthers 19th consecutive win dating back to the '87 season.

Ardsley's six game winning streak in '88 soon turned to seven with the Panthers 4-2 victory over Port Chester. Two RBIs by Matt Arone and five hits from the Caldara brothers, Jeff 3-for-4, and Tom 2-for-3, helped. Bernie McNerney snapped Port Chester's five game winning streak by scattering eight hits and striking out nine.

By April 19, Ardsley's three right handers Brian Summer, Bernie McNerney and Mike Ferraguzzi were each 2-0. But at the end of the day, Pearl River handed Ardsley and Mike Ferraguzzi its first loss of the season, 6-4.

Ardsley quickly rebounded. *Caldara Provides Welcome Relief in Ardsley's 10-7 Win,* headlined the *White Plains Reporter Dispatch* in a story about the Panthers victory over Rye High School. At Ardsley, Bernie McNerney's one-out, sixth-inning single broke a 7-7 tie. In his first pitching appearance of the season, Tom Caldara pitched two scoreless relief innings for the victory.

He cut short Rye's four run, sixth inning scoring burst in Ardsley's 10-7 victory at home. Ardsley's Brian Summer carried a 7-3 lead into the sixth but was replaced when the first two batters reached base. Vinny Fatato relieved and allowed Rye to tie the score 7-7.

That's when Coach Fitz walked to the mound, pointed to Tom Caldara at second base to come in and pitch with two on and none out. In two innings, Caldara allowed one hit, one walk, and struck out two.

In the bottom of the 6th, Steve Gyimesi singled for Ardsley and advanced to second on Brad Chenard's single. Both runners moved up a base on a fly ball before McNerney drove the winning run in with a single. Mike Ferraguzzi then doubled in two more runs.

Tom Caldara said that he always anticipated that later in a game when he was at second base he could be asked to come in at any point.

"I loved that," he said. "You want your starting pitchers to do well. However, in the back of my mind I had a little smirk, a little smile because I was ready to come in and attack. That was the great part about coming in for a short amount of time to close the game. If you have the mentality, you're like a pit bull and will come in and attack the other team for a short time. I happened to love that. You have to want the ball."

When Caldara pitched in relief, he dropped down to the side so he was throwing sidearm for the most part. He relied on two pitches, a fastball and a slider.

"It was definitely fun to be able to close a game because everything is on you," Caldara said. "I loved that part of it. But playing the infield was so much fun because you can use your athleticism, anticipating balls, going for short fly balls and diving. In the infield you run around so much. I enjoyed that the most."

Ardsley was now on a roll. No doubt, thoughts about another trip to the state championships crept into the players' minds. But first there was payback time for Ardsley. The Panthers had another shot at Pearl River, the school that handed Ardsley it's only loss of the season until then.

So in the friendly confines at Ardsley's home field Brad Chenard and Gyimesi provided all the fire power the Panthers needed. Chenard went 3-for-3 and Gyimesi went 2-for-3 including three RBI, a double and a towering home run over the left field fence. Winning pitcher Bernie McNerney went five innings and allowed four hits and struck out five.

Ardsley's next game against Byram Hills turned into a pitching duel that had everyone on the edge of their seat. Ardsley batters could not get around on Will Margiloff who fanned nine. One batter after another went down.

Then in the Ardsley sixth the Panthers turned to really old-school baseball. Mike Morel drove in Brad Chenard with a bases-loaded squeeze bunt. Steve Gyimesi matched Margiloff pitch for pitch. He struck out seven and gave up only two hits in winning 1-0. In the top of the seventh, Gyimesi got out of a bases loaded jam by getting the final hitter to ground out to shortstop Jeff Caldara.

It was much easier two days later against the same Byram Hills team. This time Ardsley won 12-0. Gyimesi was now playing left field and went 4-for-6 with two RBI while designated hitter Mike Ferraguzzi went 4-for-4 with two RBI. Ardsley took advantage of eight Byram Hills errors. Brian Summer threw a complete game three-hitter, struck out eight, and didn't allow a walk.

By now Ardsley was getting contributions from everyone up and down the lineup. The top of the order was doing the most damage and the Monday, April 26 *White Plains Reporter Dispatch* showed how much damage and where the key players ranked in the county.

	ab	r	hits	RBI	Avg
Steve Gyimesi (9th)	39	13	20	14	.510
Mike Ferraguzzi (12th)	24	7	12	4	.500
Jeff Caldara (14th)	33	13	16	14	.484

That listing provided quite a bit of fun for the trio. While Ferraguzzi and Caldara didn't talk about the listing, Gyimesi did.

"Steve was a kidder," said Caldara. "We would be taking batting practice or maybe we would all be in the outfield and Steve would give us an elbow and say, 'Hey, I just passed Jeff.' Mike or I wouldn't say anything. Steve brought the humor and levity to it. That's what I loved about him."

In Caldara's opinion, Gyimesi was the most talented teammate he played with in those two championship years of '87 and '88. He called him a five-tool guy who had tremendous speed, tremendous arm, and tremendous power.

On April 27 the Panthers crossed the Hudson River to take on Nanuet. Bernie McNerney had little trouble as he raised his pitching record to 4-0 with a two-hit, eight strikeout performance. Several days later the *New York Daily News* ranked Ardsley No. 26 in the Daily News Golden Twenty of the best teams in the New York region.

McNerney was now showing why he was one of the best pitchers in Westchester County. At Westlake he pitched a no-hitter in a League 7 matchup, striking out 10 while walking only one batter. Tom Caldara went 2-for-4 and Craig Stevens, 2-for-2, in leading the offense. McNerney was now 6-0, second in the county in wins.

However, in his next outing against arch rival Eastchester High School McNerney lost his first game of the season. Eastchester upset Ardsley 13-8 as Mickey Morgan went 2-for 3 with six RBI for the winners. Despite the loss, Ardsley players continued to wield hot bats.

Mike Ferraguzzi was second in the county in batting at .545 average, Jeff Caldara was hitting .460, Steve Gyimesi and Brad Chenard were both at .446.

The loss to Eastchester was soon forgotten. McNerney and Ardsley rebounded against Pelham. Bernie's eighth inning single scored Ferraguzzi with the winning run in a 5-4 victory. He also struck out nine in a strong complete game effort.

Four more games were left before the best of three Section 1 Class baseball championship series. Ardsley would score 53 runs in the four games and win them all.

First the Panthers trounced Edgemont, 16-3. Mike Ferraguzzi went 2-for-3 to raise his batting average to .551. Steve Gyimesi picked up the win. Then at home, all nine Ardsley starters had a hit in a 13-3 win over Briarcliff. Frank Moretti's game-winning RBI single in the fourth inning began a five-run rally. Bernie McNerney went five innings to pick up the win. Ardsley was now 20-2.

With a 4-3 win over Pine Plains Ardsley moved a little closer to a third straight Class C state title. Ardsley's fans got anxious in the top half of the seventh when Pine Plains scored twice to cut the deficit to 4-3. But reliever Mike Ferraguzzi ended the game with a strikeout. That was after Brian Summer went 6 2/3 innings to pick up his sixth win of the year.

Then in a Class C semi-final contest, Ardsley beat Rye Neck 20-5 pounding out 18 hits in the Class C semi-final contest. Bernie McNerney led the hit parade going 3-for-3 with 3 RBI. Tom Caldara was 2-for-3 including a two-run home run. Winning pitcher Steve Gyimesi went 2-for-4 with a two-run homer. He also went 5 1/3 innings striking out five while walking four.

Ardsley's most bitter rival Eastchester High School was next in the first of a three game series to decide the Section 1 Class C champions.

Few teams won as consistently or as often as the Ardsley Panthers and Eastchester Eagles in the 1980s. So when the teams took the diamond against each other it enhanced Westchester's best high school baseball rivalry.

It was something when their two Hall of Fame coaches, Dom

Cecere and Neil Fitzpatrick, went up against each other. Over a 52 year career Cecere racked up the New York State record of 737 wins for Eastchester. Fitzpatrick meanwhile over 30 years would won 306 games for Ardsley with an unequaled four consecutive state titles. In '88 they led their schools into the '88 best-of-three Section 1 Class C baseball championship series.

"Dom Cecere's the best," said Fitzpatrick. "I admired the guy so much. I had tremendous respect for him. Dom did it right. He coached very well."

However, going up against Eastchester wasn't anything special for Fitzpatrick.

"No, I fought that. I respected Dom but I felt it was very important to let our kids think that going up against Eastchester wasn't mysterious. It's baseball. I wouldn't give respect to coaches out in public. I would treat every coach the same.

"When Dom was coaching against us he was very sociable and tried to engage me in conversation. But I didn't want any part of it. I had rules for our kids, not to talk to opposition players. I liked that discipline. I recognized that just because somebody was supposed to be good I'd still say, 'Let's play the game. Let's see who is going to win today.'

"I would never save a pitcher for a particular opponent. I didn't change pitching rotations. It was whoever was ready. I never thought one team was better than another. On a given day, you can't wait for Eastchester next week. You have to beat Peekskill today. That's why we were successful against Eastchester. We never treated them as being anything special. My philosophy was that all opponents were the same."

That may have been how Coach Fitzpatrick looked at the Eastchester-Ardsley rivalry. It sure wasn't how Ardsley players viewed it or how they remember the rivalry today.

"We were Eastchester's white whale. We put a thorn in their side," said Mike Ferraguzzi, long after he played his last high school game.

For Ardsley's Jeff Caldara that rivalry started with his older brothers who played against the Eagles in football and baseball.

"For us it was Eastchester every year," he said. "No doubt there was scuttlebutt in our locker room. "We would say, 'Hey guys, this is a big game. This is a game where we have to have our A game.' It always panned out like that.

"There is no doubt that the '88 best-of-three Section 1 series games were amplified. There was more energy in the air when we played them."

Eastchester didn't help themselves in that series.

"We had beaten them in the first game of the series," Caldara said. "We were coming back to our field to play and found out that Eastchester kids came over and spray painted stuff on our dugout and on the high school wall. Once we saw that we knew we were going to win."

27. RHUBARB AND TRIP TO STATES

There are all kinds of ways to win baseball games and coaches can have a decided impact.

That's just what happened in the first game of the best-of-three Section 1 Class C baseball championship series against Eastchester High School with Ardsley's assistant coach Paul Murphy.

Ardsley was losing late in the game and Murphy was sitting on the bench near Coach Fitzpatrick. Paul didn't like what he was seeing. He thought the umpire was currying favor with Eastchester's legendary coach Dom Cecere. Heroes and baseball legends like Ted Williams can do that. Paul felt Ardsley wasn't getting any calls.

Murphy had enough and jumped out of the dugout, ran onto the field and got into the umpire's face. Paul turned his hat backwards and the umpire did the same thing. Temperatures were boiling. Paul and the umpire had at it. It was like watching former Baltimore Orioles manager Earl Weaver arguing in his prime.

Murphy was thrown out of the game. However, there was a method to Paul's madness. Everybody on the bench was talking about Murphy. The act certainly inspired Ardsley and helped the Panthers win the game.

"I looked back while Paul was arguing and saw C.J. Russo and other former Ardsley players just watching Murphy in awe and cheering him on," said Ardsley's Mike Ferraguzzi.

When the team returned to Ardsley Coach Fitz appreciated what Murphy said to him. Paul apologized. He said, "Coach, I'm sorry." With or without that apology Murphy's actions surely sparked the team.

With three runs in the top of the sixth and two more in the seventh Ardsley defeated Eastchester 7-5 in the series opening game. Eastchester had taken a 2-0 lead in the second inning but Ardsley came back to tie it in the third when Steve Gyimesi doubled and Jeff Caldara hit a two-out, two-run homer to right field. Three singles and two wild pitches served up by Eastchester reliever Butch Burrough led to two more Ardsley runs in the seventh.

Gyimesi led off that rally with a single. He moved to second on a wild pitch and scored on an RBI single by Brad Chenard. Brad then advanced to second on a wild pitch and Caldara drove him home with a line-drive double to center.

"We wanted to get up and hit the ball hard wherever it was pitched and get the first guy on," said Chenard in a *White Plains Reporter Dispatch* story. "I was looking for a fastball. I zoned it. I'm a low fastball hitter. We jump on the heat."

Murphy's antics took place late in the game. Ardsley entered the sixth inning trailing by three runs and then put runners on first and second. Bernie McNerney, who went the distance for the victory, singled to score Caldara from second, with pinch runner Vinny Fatato going to third.

After McNerney stole second and left fielder Mike Morel struck out, Matt Arone ripped an 0-2 pitch for a single, scoring Fatato. It was one of Arone's biggest hits of the year. Frank Moretti's sacrifice fly then scored McNerney to tie the game at 5-5 and eventually led to Ardsley's win.

The second game of the series was scheduled for Saturday at Ardsley. Rain started falling before it began while both teams sat on their benches glaring at each other. The night before Eastchester fans spray painted both dugouts with signs "Eastchester Rules" and "Ardsley Out". The game was called off before the first pitch. That evening the Ardsley boys had time to talk about it at Mike Ferraguzzi's barbeque.

Two days later the headline in the *White Plains Reporter Dispatch* read "Ferraguzzi Hits and Pitches Champs Past Eastchester, 12-5". Ferraguzzi, Ardsley's designated hitter relief pitcher, was a busy man in the win. At bat, he led his team with three RBI and two doubles. On the mound he worked 3 1/3 innings in relief to pick up the win while allowing one run. Ardsley had now won its fourth consecutive Section 1 Class C baseball championship with this 12-5 victory of visiting Eastchester.

The Panthers scored all the runs they needed in the first two innings. Brad Chenard's RBI double in the first reduced the Eastchester lead to 2-1. Jeff Caldara flied out to left field with runners at second and third however the outfielder's throw to the plate went out of play allowing Steve Gyimesi to score from third and Chenard from second. That gave Ardsley the lead for good, 3-2. Ferraguzzi's two-run double to center field finished the scoring in a four-run second inning. Ardsley's lead was now 7-2.

The Eagles did threaten in the fourth when a two-out rally produced a pair of runs, closing the Eastchester deficit to 7-4. After a walk loaded the bases, starter Brian Summer, who at one point had retired 10 consecutive batters, was relieved by Ferraguzzi. Mickey Morgan flied out to center fielder Frank Moretti to end the threat and Ferraguzzi retired the last six batters he faced.

Next up for Ardsley, now 24-2, was an intersectional game against Marlboro High in Montgomery, NY. An Ardsley win there would punch the team's ticket to the New York State Baseball championships on Saturday in Little Falls.

It was a windy day on June 6 in Montgomery when Ardsley began 1988 intersectional play against Section 9 champ Marlboro High. As soon as Ardsley's players saw Marlboro's starting pitcher warming up they knew he was mediocre at best.

Jeff Caldara remembers standing next to Mike Ferraguzzi and Steve Gyimesi. They felt confident and thought that it would be a pretty good day. Jeff's brother Tom led the game off with a hit. That was just the beginning.

While most teams take batting practice before a game, Ardsley spent more than two hours taking batting practice against three Marlboro pitchers. The result was a 25-hit outbreak in the Panthers 21-7 win in the opening round of intersectional play.

"The confidence we felt just watching what was going on, the field, the atmosphere, what we had done in the past, we knew we were going to get to the regional finals," said Jeff Caldara who went 5-for-5 for the first time that season.

The Panthers led 5-2 going into the top of the fifth when it put the game away for good. With one out, Ardsley had seven straight hits. Two run singles by third baseman Bernie McNerney, catcher Matt Arone, and second baseman Tom Caldara aided the 8-run, eight hit attack.

An inning later, Ardsley used the long ball to duplicate its fifth-inning outbreak. Center fielder Frank Moretti's three-run homer over the right center field fence, Jeff Caldara's two run shot to dead center and Mike Ferraguzzi's solo home run padded the lead.

Every Ardsley starter got at least two hits and an RBI except for winning pitcher Steve Gyimesi. Besides Jeff Caldara, McNerney (4-for-4, two RBI) was perfect at the plate. What made Coach Fitzpatrick particularly proud was that the bottom third of the order, Mike Morel, Matt Arone and Frank Moretti, went 9-for-15.

Gyimesi threw 4 2/3 innings and allowed a pair of home runs by catcher John Conte. The second homer was a grand slam with two outs in the fifth inning. Conte's first homer in the fourth provided the game's most bizarre play.

Conte blasted a shot to left field which bounced over the fence. Conte didn't stop at second base. Instead he circled the bases for a two-run homer which cut the Ardsley lead to 5-2. The three umpires failed to notice the bounce, and did not order Conte to return to second base. Although he gave up two home runs, Gyimesi allowed one hit in his first three innings of work. Tom Caldara pitched the final two innings giving up one run on two hits and retiring the last five batters he faced. Tom also had four RBIs.

After it was all over, Ardsley was 25-2 and had to face Long Island Class C Champion Mattituck of Section 11 Suffolk County in the Southeast Regional final. A win would earn a trip for the boys to the state championships for the third year in a row.

And who better to secure that trip than Ardsley's ace right hander Bernie McNerney who was a big admirer of Boston Red Sox hurler Roger Clemens. Bernie liked the way Clemens overpowered people.

That's what Bernie liked to do as well and he did just that, tossing a three-hit shutout while striking out 10 as the Panthers beat Mattituck High School 3-0 at Port Chester's Rec Park.

McNerney was unbeatable that day, walking only one batter while using an occasional curve ball along with his fastball. He threw 105 pitches and faced only four batters over the minimum. He also gave up only three fly ball outs.

His teammate Mike Ferraguzzi, who had seen Bernie at his best, said this performance was even better than Bernie's no-hitter against Westlake earlier in the season.

Mattituck offered its only threat in the fifth inning when a walk followed by single put runners on at first and second. Coach Fitzpatrick made a trip to the mound for a conference with Bernie but never thought about taking him out of the game. A fly out and strikeout ended the inning.

Ferraguzzi went 2 for 3 with an RBI for Ardsley while teammate Steve Gyimesi doubled over the center fielder's head and later tripled into the left field corner. After the game Gyimesi was the first to say that Ardsley could win it all if it played its game and not make mistakes.

Going into the state championships Ardsley had everything. That included an explosive lineup, great defense, three solid starting pitchers and a designated hitter Mike Ferraguzzi who could be called on to pitch relief.

Before the state championships began Ferraguzzi was leading the team with a .551 batting average. Shortstop Jeff Caldara led with five home runs, 35 RBI and 38 runs scored. His brother Tom was hitting .355 in the leadoff spot. Gyimesi was a strong No. 2 hitter. No. 3 hitter Brad Chenard was batting .382. The bottom of the order provided a welcome offense with Mike Morel, Matt Arone and Frank Moretti going a combined 28 for 63 (.444) in seven postseason games.

Ardsley's pitching was solid. Junior Bernie McNerney (9-1, 3.41 ERA, 56 strikeouts and 23 walks) was Ardsley's stopper. Brian Summer's strength (6-0, 2.15 ERA) was a pinpoint curve that baffled many tough hitters and Steve Gyimesi (4-0) featured a scary sidearm delivery. Ferraguzzi was the primary closer for these starting pitchers.

Ardsley's team bus would soon leave for upstate New York.

28. MCNERNEY BRILLIANT
IN SEMIFINAL WIN

Ardsley had only a few days to savor its southeastern regional title before leaving for a four hour 230 mile bus ride to Utica for the Class C state semifinal game.

An overcast and humid day greeted the team when it arrived at a high school upstate for a practice before checking into a hotel.

Appropriately the batting practice screen, balls and bats were the first things that came out of the bus. There was very little talking. Everyone knew their role. Once the field was set up Coach Fitz started throwing BP. The only noise was a bat hitting a ball.

The atmosphere was definitely different than regular season practices. It was more businesslike than usual. Captain Jeff Caldara didn't have to say anything to his teammates. They knew what had to be done.

Years later, Coach Fitzpatrick said that Jeff made sure that the players took their duties seriously, that the practice went well and all the equipment was transferred properly. "That was an amazing performance. I could not have asked for an assistant coach to do more," he said. "In addition, Jeff played like a Most Valuable Player.

"Bernie McNerney, maybe Ardsley's best pitcher ever, was voted MVP for his extraordinary pitching. But Jeff, both defensively and offensively, and as our captain was truly as good as an athlete can be."

After practice the bus was loaded and players climbed aboard for the short trip to the hotel. Again, there was very little conversation when the youngsters checked in, showered and went to dinner. They were ready. Nothing had to be said by Coach Fitz or the captains.

On Saturday morning, Coach Fitzpatrick had a master plan for his team before the game. The players awoke at 6 am. Following breakfast at 6:45, the team went through a 45 minute practice. The team finally arrived at Utica's Murnane Field at 8:45. Stepping off the bus onto Murnane's cut grass the boys stopped for a moment, taking it all in. For some it didn't matter that they played ball there before. This was a ballpark they would never forget.

More infield and outfield practice followed before a mid-morning semi-final game against Central Region champion St. Lawrence Central.

"We knew what we had to do," said Ardsley leadoff hitter Tom Caldara in a *White Plains Reporter Dispatch* interview after the game. "There were no surprises. I was up for the game and not tired at all. Coach Fitzpatrick is always thinking baseball. He always takes care of us."

As 10 am game time approached, cars pulled up and unloaded the Ardsley faithful. About 300 folks made the trip north. That cheering crowd was an intangible that the players appreciated.

On the mound Bernie McNerney put on his glove. He started throwing practice pitches. Coach Fitzpatrick was watching and surely felt good about his decision to start his ace. McNerney. who would become the tournament most valuable player, was getting ready and perhaps thought about just one thing. *Ok St. Lawrence. This is what I've got. Try hitting it.*

McNerney was pitching on just three days' rest. That didn't matter. He was brilliant, striking out 11 while walking one. He painted the corner with his fastball and completely confused the St. Lawrence batters with his curve. Strike three. Strike three. Strike three. Bernie struck out the side in the first inning and retired the first 10 batters he faced.

McNerney even had a "K Korner" in the stands behind home plate that noted each strikeout.

After the game he admitted that this 2-1 win over St. Lawrence

Central was definitely one of the best games he had ever pitched. A couple of days earlier he tossed a complete game three-hit shutout against Mattituck to win the Southeast Regional.

In the seventh and last inning against St. Lawrence McNerney even started thinking about a no-hitter. That wishful thinking ended when he gave up a home run. After that homer McNerney got the next two outs and then struck out a batter to apparently end the game. However, the pitch was in the dirt and got away from catcher Matt Arone, allowing the batter to reach first. A popup to Brad Chenard in foul territory near first base ended the game and Ardsley was in the state finals again.

Runs weren't plentiful for Ardsley that morning. The Panthers took a 1-0 lead in the fifth against St. Lawrence. With two outs and Frank Moretti on third base, Brad Chenard hit a 1-2 pitch off the left-center field wall for a triple, scoring Moretti.

What proved to be the game winning run for the Panthers came in the sixth. With one out and runners on second and third, Arone perfectly executed a suicide squeeze, scoring pinch-runner Vinny Fatato from third.

Coach Neil Fitzpatrick's record during the past four years was now 97-9. McNerney ended the '88 season 10-1. Ardsley had one more game to play in but a few hours.

29. CHAMPS MEET GOVERNOR MARIO CUOMO

A few hours after edging St. Lawrence in the Class C state semifinal game Ardsley even joined an illustrious list of major league teams, the New York Yankees and Oakland Athletics, that won three championships in row.

The Panthers survived a seventh-inning rally by Far West champion JFK Cheektowaga to come away with an 8-4 win and its third straight Class C state title. For history buffs, Cheektowaga's earliest known occupants were the Iroquois and later the Seneca Indians. The town is in Erie County and is Buffalo's second largest suburb.

As the game wore on Ardsley starter Brian Summer had thoughts of duplicating Bernie McNerney's semifinal performance when a few hours earlier Bernie threw six innings of no hit ball in winning 2-1.

Summer pitched six innings of two-hit shutout baseball. All he needed to do was shutdown Cheektowaga in the seventh and Ardsley would win the states. There was one problem. Brian gave up five consecutive hits that closed the Ardsley lead to 8-4.

During that rally Coach Fitzpatrick didn't have anyone warming up in the Panthers bullpen. He usually would turn to Mike Ferraguzzi. Players on the bench were looking at each and wondering what was happening. Coach Fitz didn't have Mike in the bullpen.

Finally, Paul Murphy looked at Coach Fitz and said he was taking Guzzi out to the bullpen. Coach Fitz agreed with that. Interestingly, when Coach Fitz forgot something that is the only time Murphy would get in there to help.

Coach Fitz finally walked out to the mound and made a sign to the bullpen. His call was for Ferraguzzi. Just as he did a year earlier, Ferraguzzi was summoned to seal the victory. A ground out and then strike three and strike three again. Mike saved the day again. At that moment the Ardsley boys' lives were changed. They were state champions again. Besides his pitching heroics, Ferraguzzi had a major impact on the '88 championship in another way. His two run double in the first inning helped give Ardsley a 4-0 lead. Ferraguzzi said it was even better in '88 when he got a groundout and two strikeouts to end the game.

Ardsley jumped ahead with runs in the first inning as the first five Panther batters reached base. In the second inning, Steve Gyimesi's two-out single drove home Frank Moretti to give the champions a 5-0 lead. Jeff Caldara's two-out single in the fourth inning scored Matt Arone and Tom Caldara to increase the lead to 7-0. Arone's one-out RBI triple in the fifth capped the scoring.

Jeff Caldara recalls coming back on the bus from states in '87 and '88 and as the team was getting closer to the high school, *"We Are The Champions"* was blaring on a tape recorder. "Pulling up to your parents and to people who were ready to pick you up was the first time we really had a chance to talk to them," he said. "We would see them passing in the stadium. This was the first time however when the players had a chance to embrace and talk. We saw their emotions and how they felt and what the experience meant to them."

Soon the now familiar motorcade through town. It took off from the Ardsley Middle School at 11 am and proceeded along Ashford Avenue to Route 9A, north to Heatherdell Road, right to Farm Road and on to the high school.

A few days later the 19 members of the team had their own history lesson about New York State when they visited Albany and met with then Governor Mario Cuomo who was a pretty good ballplayer himself. The governor saw time in 81 games with the Class D Minor League Brunswick Pirates during the 1952 season. A 20-year-old center fielder with the club, Cuomo hit .244 with a total of 62 hits, including one home run and 10 doubles. He quickly realized his career wasn't going to play out on the diamond.

On this day in Albany with the Ardsley team gathered around him, the governor asked who the best hitter on the team was. A couple of teammates shouted "Ferraguzzi". Cuomo was impressed with Mike's .551 batting average and encouraged him to sit in his governor's chair which Ferraguzzi did. He was surrounded by his teammates including his fellow All Section 1 team members Jeff Caldara and Bernie McNerney.

Before leaving on a yellow school bus for Albany Fitzpatrick had T-shirts made up for his players listing their league, sectional and state titles. It also contained his motto, "All 21 outs."

After the Albany visit more honors would come Ardsley's way. *USA Today* reported on June 22 about the top high school baseball teams in the country. The final Easton Sports /Collegiate Baseball National High School Baseball Poll ranked Ardsley as the 14th best high school baseball team in the nation after compiling a 28-2 record.

A.H.S. Baseball Champs 1988 — Bottom Row: (Left to Right) J. Fanelli, J. Meinel, T. Caldara, T. J. Rau, D. Chenard. Middle Row: M. Ferraguzzi, J. Caldara, B. Chenard, F. Moretti, S. Gyimesi, M. Morel. Back Row: V. Fatato, J. Gruning, B. McNerney, C. Stephens, B. Summer, M. Good, M. Arone. Missing: M. Scallero.

Bernie McNerney with a 25-2 career record called by Coach Fitzpatrick his greatest pitcher.

Bernie McNerney

Jeff Caldara led '88 team with five home runs, 37 RBI, 39 runs scored, and named state tournament MVP.

By the end of 2018 Jeff Caldara finished his 21st season as Ardsley's baseball coach, four more years than Coach Fitzpatrick's tenure.

Photo of second baseman Tom Caldara, left, and brother Jeff his shortstop, called by Coach Fitzpatrick a picture to cherish.

Michael Ferraguzzi, left, and Brad Chenard with '88 New York State trophy.

Fans in the Ardsley stands in '88.

'88 team introduced at state championship tournament.

Home plate from state championship field.

A winning motorcade ritual at '88 season's end.

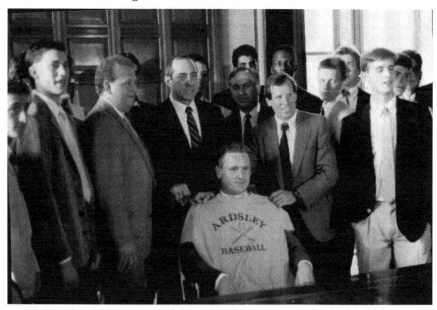

Governor Mario Cuomo asked who was the best hitter on the team. Teammates shouted Ferraguzzi and Michael got a seat in the governor's chair.

Coach Neil Fitzpatrick, left, Assemblyman Richard Brodsky, players Jeff Caldara, Brad Chenard and Frank Moretti, second from right, present New York Governor Mario Cuomo with a 1988 baseball T-shirt. Looking on at far right is Senator Nicholas Spano.

Time to revise sign on high school wall near baseball field after championship '88 season.

1989

30. IGNORING THE PAST FOCUSING ON THE PRESENT

How good could the Ardsley Panthers be in 1989 after coming off a 28-2 season while winning the Class C New York State championship for the third year in a row?

For starters, Jeff Caldara, Brad Chenard, Brian Summer, Mike Ferraguzzi, Frank Moretti and Matt Arone had graduated. In years past, new talent had always filled the space. Coach Fitzpatrick's '89 team would be no different. Newcomers like Jordan Polvere, Tom Ferraguzzi, Dave Chenard and T.J. Rau would make an impact.

The biggest contributors however would be a trio of Ardsley returning lettermen, Bernie McNerney, Steve Gyimesi and Tom Caldara. At least one of the three would play a major role in virtually all of the Panther wins in '89. All three would be named First Team All-County. Besides these three Mike Morel and Craig Stephens would see plenty of playing time.

Then there was Coach Neil Fitzpatrick. In his memoirs about his athletic career he wrote, "That by the time we had won three New York State championships in a row it was difficult to keep my healthy perspective. I was actually looking forward so much to when the string would be broken. But of course that would be so unfair to want a team you are coaching to lose so that I could get some peace from all this attention I was getting."

That may have been Fitzpatrick's thoughts years after he retired but those thoughts didn't change the way he coached in '89. He made sure there was no complacency and for sure didn't let past success have an impact.

And that may be the key ingredient for all of Ardsley's success as Section 1's team of the decade in the eighties. The Panthers ignored the past and just focused on the present. That is hard to do. Keeping a one-game-at-a-time attitude epitomized all his championship teams. They didn't think about past victories or worry about living up to their reputation.

Now in his ninth year as coach, Fitzpatrick downplayed any discussion about earlier glory. He didn't compare the '89 Panthers to any of his past teams.

"The past just gets in the way. This year is all that counts," Fitzpatrick said in a *White Plains Reporter Dispatch* story midway during the '89 season. "There's no such thing as an upset in baseball because on any given day any team can beat you. Baseball is the one sport where you are what you are that day. Baseball is a game of repetition and of game situations. It's not like pulling teeth to have good practices. We have good players who are willing to get better.

"What's important is that the only thing we have control over is what we do on a day-to-day basis. All the other stuff like league, sectional and state titles take care of itself."

"The fact that we've won state championships means that everybody is coming after us," Tom Caldara said in the same article. "All of us just work hard, and we're out practicing harder than last year. We just play ball every day and play our hearts out."

That's when Coach Fitz started thinking about his opening day lineup. Taking the departed Brad Chenard's place at first base was lefty Jordan Polvere. Jordan's father planted him at first when he was seven or eight years old and he never left. As preteens, he and catcher Tommy Ferraguzzi were linked forever.

"It was almost telepathic between the two of us," said Ferraguzzi. "There would be men on first and second base. The guy leading off first would sometimes get cocky because he thought there was no way a catcher was going to throw behind the runner.

"Jordan at first would pretend he wasn't paying attention. He would take his hat and throw it up in the air and try to catch it on his head. This was all intended to lull the runner into a false sense of security. Jordan would then sneak back in close to the bag and I would throw a strike to get him out. We did that a number of times during the '89 season."

Moving over to centerfield in '89 was Mike Morel a character for sure but as dependable an outfielder as they come. Coach Paul Murphy called Morel the "Mayor of LaLa Land" because Murphy would look to the outfield and watch Morel throwing his hat in the air while trying to catch it on his head. Even today scores of players from that era could be named while Mike's name probably would rarely come up.

Dave Chenard followed in his brother Brad's footsteps. Coach Fitz's new left fielder had the best arm in the outfield and showed it off during pre-game practices. Dave was the fellow who would always grab the rake to groom the batter's box when it was wet before batting practice.

On the left side of the infield Craig Stephens was back for another season at third base. Many people thought he should have been the MVP of the '88 state tournament because of his defensive play.

Next to Stephens was T.J. Rau at shortstop who would soon blossom into a quality pitcher. Rau was driven to be good. He was quiet and did his own thing. He was part of the same social fabric as the rest of his teammates and would go out after games to parties but he didn't run in the same social circles that many of his teammates did.

It may be hard to imagine how Tom Caldara could improve on his '88 season when he hit .353. He surely did.

An important part of the folklore of baseball is the significance attached to pitching in winning games. In '89 Ardsley had the best one-two pitching combination in Westchester County in Bernie McNerney and Steve Gyimesi.

They were different pitchers. Bernie was more traditional pitching from over the top. He had a curve ball that broke 12 to 6. He worked the corners. He was a power pitcher but super smart and super competitive. He rarely walked anybody. He was a man among the boys. He was the unofficial leader of the team, the alpha dog. He didn't have to say anything to prove it. His teammates knew it.

Tommy Ferraguzzi who caught both pitchers called Bernie a bulldog and points to the fact that Bernie as a sophomore was mowing guys down. Ferraguzzi recalls how Bernie did not want to talk to anybody on the mound.

"He was nasty," Ferraguzzi said. "God forbid Coach Fitz told me to go out and talk to him. Once I got to the mound he would say, 'Don't tell me what to do. I'm fine. Go back there and let me strike this guy out.'"

Bernie took a page out of Hall of Famer Bob Gibson's playbook. Gibson was respected as a great pitcher but also because he was mean, tough, a symbol of badass. Ferraguzzi had to know how Gibson's catcher Tim McCarver must have felt when he went to the mound when Gibson was pitching and was quickly told to get back behind the plate.

"Bernie was the ultimate competitor," said his second baseman Tom Caldara. "If I saw it coming where Bernie had to slow down and I could see catcher Tommy Ferraguzzi walking out, I would shake my head at second base and think to myself that it was not a good idea Tommy.

"Bernie was going to tell him to just get the hell out of there. Bernie was so feisty, so focused and so darn good."

Steve Gyimesi was Coach Fitzpatrick's number two pitcher. He came from three quarters and he threw as hard as anybody. A wicked slider and curveball were part of his repertoire. Batters didn't want to dig in when facing Gyimesi. He may not have had as much control as Bernie but talent wise there were times when he was completely unhittable.

"Steve had more of a live arm," said Ferraguzzi. "He didn't know where it was going sometimes. He was a lot more difficult to catch. With Bernie you just put the glove out and boom, boom, boom. Steve was like a right fielder with a live arm that would get you. He was undefeated in two years."

While Ardsley players weren't all great athletes, Steve Gyimesi was great. He was wiry, so athletic and exuded confidence. He looked like a professional right fielder.

When T.J. Rau pitched that's when Ardsley had its most intimidating defense. Teams could not believe the size of the team. Before Ardsley took the field before games teams were already intimidated. Bernie McNerney at 6'3" played shorstop. Craig Stephens at 6'4" held down third. Dave Chenard at 6'4" was in left field. Steve Gyimesi at 6'2" was in right field. Mike Morel and Jordan Polvere would go on to play college football while Tommy Caldara looked like a professional second baseman.

Ardsley was now ready to begin the '89 campaign and a chance to rewrite the record books even more.

31. BEST BATTER-PITCHER MATCHUP

On April 7, after more than a month of practice, Ardsley opened its '89 season with a convincing 18-4 win over Irvington in the opening round of the Irvington Hudson River Tournament.

Bernie McNerney, who went 10-1 in 1988 as a junior, picked up where he left off. A leadoff triple to left centerfield in the fourth inning broke up his no-hitter. He threw fastball after fastball in striking out ten. The Panthers' Jordan Polvere, in his varsity debut, hit an inside-the-park, three-run home run.

Four days later at home, Ardsley fans and opposing teams saw what Tom Caldara had in store for them all season long. In Ardsley's 15-8 win over Valhalla, Tom went 4 for 4, had five RBI, scored four runs and stole two bases. Two of his hits were home runs. Steve Gyimesi picked up his first win of the season.

McNerney won twice more the following week followed by junior T.J. Rau's win at home against Tappan Zee. Rau limited the visitors to one unearned run on four hits in his first varsity start. Ardsley then went to 6-0 with a 7-3 win over Edgemont.

The Panthers extended their winning streak to 19 games with a victory over Roslyn, 16-6. Coach Fitzpatrick turned to Dave Chenard to pitch his first varsity game. The Ardsley bats came alive with Tom Caldara going 4 for 5 including three RBI while Bernie McNerney, Jordan Polvere and Chenard each had multiple hit games.

By now the Panthers' record dating back to 1987 was 56-6. However, Ardsley then got a scare in its lowest run producing game of the '89 season, a 1-0 victory on the road over Peekskill. The

Panthers needed Bernie McNerney's 13-strikeout, two-hit performance. Craig Stephens tripled home Steve Gyimesi with two out in the fifth inning for the game's only run.

Peekskill would get another chance three days later. An eight column newspaper banner headline told about the game's outcome, *Gyimesi Pitches, Hits Ardsley to 15-5 Victory*. Steve helped his own cause with four RBI including a two run home run over the left centerfield fence. Tom Caldara continued his hot early season hitting. After the win he was 20 for 36 and had a .556 batting average.

By now all Ardsley eyes were on Eastchester, an opponent with deep baseball heritage and the coach with the most wins in Westchester County baseball history, Dom Cecere. Back to back games would give one team bragging rights.

In the opener, T.J. Rau's second homer of the day broke a 3-3 tie in the sixth inning for a 4-3 Ardsley win. Bernie McNerney went all the way while striking out 13 in gaining his fifth win of the season.

A few days later, the Eastchester team arrived at Ardsley High School for a rematch. On the sidelines warming up for the Eagles was Butch Burrough, a flame thrower who was mentioned in the same breath with Bernie McNerney and Steve Gyimesi. He would face Steve on this day.

For six innings fans and players alike sat on the edge of their seats watching two of the better teams and pitchers in Westchester go at it. Ardsley versus Eastchester. Gyimesi versus Burrough.

Then the bottom of the seventh inning arrived. Earlier in the seventh, Eastchester tied the score. Then with one out in a tie game, Ardsley's designated hit T.J. Rau, who was hitting ninth in the order, walked and stole second base. Then Tom Caldara grabbed his 33 inch 30 ounce Easton bat and strode to the plate to face Burrough.

It was mano a mano. Baseball fans may recall the best pitcher-hitter rivalries, Ted Williams versus Bob Feller; Willie Mays and Hank Aaron versus Bob Gibson or Sandy Koufax; Mike Schmidt versus Nolan Ryan; and Barry Bonds versus Greg Maddox or Randy Johnson. While it is not in that class, at the high school level it was Caldara versus Burrough.

With each step towards the batter's box Tom kept thinking about what his father Bart had always told him, hit the ball up the middle and make solid contact and don't try to do too much.

On the mound Burrough rocked and delivered pitch after pitch. The count went to 3-2. Butch then threw a fastball towards the outside corner of the plate. Tom reacted. He swung and hit a rope that was just a couple of feet off the ground. It kept carrying and hit off the middle of the wall at the right field foul pole. Tom's RBI double drove in the winning run in Ardsley's and Gyimesi's 3-2 victory.

After the game, Tom's father Bart and Eastchester coach Dom Cecere spoke to each other. They had known one another for many years.

Dom was asked why he hadn't walked Bart's son Tom since first base was open. "Dom told my dad that he didn't because he wanted to see the best, Butch against Tom," Caldara said. "That was one game you'll never forget, particularly because of those comments Dom Cecere shared with my dad."

By now Tom Caldara had a .591 batting average and had driven in 20 runs. The team was riding a 23 game winning streak. The Panthers had a 91 percent won-loss mark (60-6) dating back to 1987. That included a 17-0 postseason record.

On the mound and as an outfielder, Steve Gyimesi was batting .484 with 16 RBI and a 4-0 pitching record. Senior Bernie McNerney had five victories to lead the county in wins. And maybe the best No. 7 hitter in Section 1 catcher Tom Ferraguzzi sported a .433 average.

Midway through the season, Gyimesi was one of 16 players selected to participate on the U.S. High School All-Star District One baseball squad that would travel to Japan and Hawaii in July.

In the first week of May Bernie McNerney recorded his second shutout of the season in beating Nanuet, 4-0. Next on the schedule were back to back games against the Pelham Pelicans. In a low scoring game at Ardsley, Mike Morel's single in the bottom of the fifth inning drove in the go-ahead runs in a 4-2 victory. Steve Gyimesi raised his record to 5-0 and Ardsley was now 14-0.

Two days later, Ardsley tasted defeat for the first time in the '89 season losing to Pelham High School, 9-8. Its 26 game winning streak was snapped as well. The Pelicans won the game with two runs in the bottom of the eighth inning after Ardsley had gone ahead in the top of the eighth on an RBI single by Steve Gyimesi. Tom Caldara took the loss.

The next day in school Tom Ferraguzzi was walking with classmate John Tucker. Coach Fitzpatrick passed by and baseball came up in the discussion. Tucker said to Coach Fitz, "It's probably a good thing that you lost that first game." He said that because he felt the loss would take the pressure off the team.

Coach Fitz looked at Tucker and said, "What do you mean?" Tucker tried to explain. Coach Fitz said, "I don't get what you're saying." Coach Fitzpatrick refused to acknowledge that anything good could come from a loss.

Then to the surprise of almost everyone who followed Ardsley baseball, Westlake handed Ardsley its second loss in a row in beating the Panthers 7-6. Few Ardsley faithful could remember the last time the Panthers had lost two games in a row.

Later in the week, Ardsley bounced back by beating Byram Hills, 12-2, behind Steve Gyimesi's seven-strikeout pitching.

Ardsley now needed two more victories to clinch the League III-A championship. The first win came when Ardsley used four pitchers who combined on a two-hitter to defeat Sleepy Hollow 9-2 in the championship game of the Irvington Hudson River Tournament.

Winning pitcher Steve Gyimesi relieved starter Jordan Polvere in the third inning and picked up the win. Tom Caldara blasted a two-out, three-run homer to left field in the seventh inning to put the game away. He also pitched the sixth inning and Bernie McNerney retired the Headless Horsemen in order in the seventh.

Ardsley then won its fourth league championship in the previous five years with a 8-0 shutout of Nanuet. Craig Stephens went 2 for 3 with four RBI while winning pitcher Bernie McNerney went the distance, striking out 11, and going 2-for-4 including two RBI.

It was now time for T.J. Rau to show his stuff in a preview of what fans would see in the year ahead. He pitched a two-hit complete game shutout, his first of the season, in defeating Byram Hills 9-0. Both Bernie McNerney and Steve Gyimesi drove in three runs.

The Class C tournament awaited Ardsley.

32. SEVENTH INNING RALLIES DO THE JOB

News traveled fast around Ardsley where its high school baseball team had become a tremendous source of pride for everyone living in the village. The Panthers were about to take on Edgemont High School in a Class C quarterfinal contest on Monday, May 29 at home.

Every game now seemed like an elimination contest. For all Ardsley seniors a loss would mean an end to their high school careers. Keep winning and capturing another New York State title and Ardsley would add to its growing legacy.

With the '89 season winding down, competition was getting tougher. It took Ardsley six innings against Edgemont to finally come up with the game-winner, a Jordan Polvere double that scored Tom Caldara. Caldara and Steve Gyimesi each went 2-for-3 while Bernie McNerney hurled another complete game to pick up the win.

Next up for the Panthers was Nanuet High School in a Class C semifinal contest at home. This time it only took Ardsley one inning to put the game away. The team scored 10 runs on four hits in which 14 players batted. Steve Gyimesi went six innings to pick up the 17-0 win and also tie McNerney with a 7-0 pitching record.

Big games were now on Ardsley's schedule. That's why Ardsley fans may have been a little surprised when Coach Fitzpatrick turned to T.J. Rau to start the first game of the best-of-three Section 1 Class C championship against Pine Plains. If those fans had known how Neil Fitzpatrick coached they wouldn't have been surprised at all. It was Rau's turn to start. He was up in the rotation and besides McNerney was tired from all the innings he had thrown.

"I would never save anybody," said Coach Fitz. " I didn't change pitching rotations. It was whoever was ready."

T.J. was ready and he didn't disappoint. He went 6 2/3 innings, struck out four and walked four in a 5-2 win.

One thing Coach Fitz always preached was 'do it with two', meaning he would like the team to score when there were two outs and nobody on base. "If your team can get a run then that's incredible," he said.

So when Ardsley staged a two-out rally in the third Coach Fitz was surely impressed. Following a Tom Caldara triple, Jordan Polvere's RBI single gave the Panthers a 1-0 lead. Then Gyimesi walked and Craig Stephens came through with a two run double which gave Ardsley a 3-0 lead and all the runs it needed.

In the second game of this best-of-three series, Bernie McNerney was still under the weather when he took the mound against Pine Plains. Ardsley fans and Pine Plains batters would never have known that with the way he pitched. McNerney threw a one-hitter and faced two batters over the minimum in Ardsley's 17-1 win. He relied on his fastball and curve throughout the game.

"Winning the sectionals isn't automatic for us, but we know this is the time of year when playing well really counts," McNerney told *The White Plains Reporter Dispatch.* "I think we've got a legitimate shot at winning the states again, but with single elimination you never know."

In the fourth inning Tom Ferraguzzi hit a three-run home run to center field that gave Ardsley a 9-1 lead.

"That was the only home run I ever hit in high school," Ferraguzzi said. "I have the ball downstairs in my house. It was more a long fly ball to right center. I hit it perfectly. My dad and Mr. Caldara would always stand by themselves at the games. They didn't want to talk to anybody and they didn't want anybody to talk to them.

"I remember my dad say that as soon as I hit it, Mr. Caldara said, 'That's gone.' I have pictures my mom took of me stepping on home plate with my teammates pummeling me. My brother Mike got the ball from a youngster and brought it to me after the game. I still have the ball in my basement."

The Pine Plains win pushed Ardsley's post-season record since 1987 to 21-0 and its total record since 1985 to 119-11.

The road to the state championship was still a rough one for Ardsley since the Panthers had to face Section 9 champ Chester at Brewster High School in a Class C Southeastern Region semifinal.

Again it all fell on the shoulders of leadoff second baseman Tom Caldara in the seventh inning to save the season. His no-out, RBI single to right field scored Mike Morel from third to tie the game 4-4. Then when Chester's right fielder booted the ball, T.J. Rau was sent home with the winning run. Steve Gyimesi picked up his ninth win of the season without a loss.

The seventh inning rally began with singles by Mike Morel and Rau. Dave Chenard's sacrifice bunt was fielded by Chester's first baseman who tried to force Morel at third. The third baseman dropped the ball for an error, leaving the Panthers with the bases loaded and none out.

"That was one of the most intense moments that I recall of all those years because we were on the verge of being ousted," Caldara said. "I remember being on double deck and things were getting closer for me to come to bat. Then I remember being on deck and just praying that they would get to me and that my at bat would come."

In a *White Plains Reporter Dispatch* interview after the game Caldara said, "When I got up to the plate, I just said 'Base hit up the middle' over and over again to myself.'"

Meanwhile up until then Chester pitcher Gary Lang had Caldara's number. Tom had gone 0 for 3. Caldara wasn't the only Panther befuddled by Lang. His teammates were no-hit for more than five innings.

By the time Caldara got comfortable in the batter's box he had forgotten about his previous at bats. That's when Lang rocked and delivered. "I think it was on the first pitch on the outside corner. I slashed it between first and second base. It was a quick short swing. I don't remember all that many at bats. I remember that one."

The win was emblematic of how Ardsley played throughout the season. The Panthers performed in the clutch. The last eight Panther batters in the game all reached base. Before that however the Chester

Hambletonians took a 4-3 lead in the top of the seventh with a two out rally before Caldara's game winning heroics.

Next up for the Panthers was a trip to Hampton Bays High School on Long Island for a game against Center Moriches, the Section 11 champions. At stake was the Southeastern Region title and a bus ride to the state championships in Utica, New York.

Now for the second game in a row, Ardsley waited until the last inning of regulation play, the seventh, to win the game. That's when the Panthers scored seven runs on five hits to seal the victory, 12-7.

Ardsley's barrage began when clean-up hitter Craig Stephens singled and moved to second on a wild pitch. Winning pitcher Bernie McNerney helped his own cause with an RBI single that gave Ardsley a 6-4 lead. After Tom Ferraguzzi's single sent McNerney to third base, Mike Morel hit a two run single over second base.

Ardsley wasn't finished yet. T.J. Rau smashed an RBI triple. Dave Chenard and Tom Caldara walked to load the bases. Ardsley then had a 10-4 lead on Jordan Polvere's sacrifice fly. The Panthers final two runs came across on an error by the centerfielder.

McNerney, now 10-0 for the season, went 6 1/3 innings while pitching on only two days rest. He admitted he was just burned out. That's when Coach Fitzpatrick called on Caldara to close out the game. Tom gave up to two singles and then fanned the next batter for the second out. All he needed was one more out for a trip to states. That's when Caldara took a deep breath and fired. Strike three. The Panthers were headed to Utica for their fourth consecutive berth in the state baseball championships.

33. FOUR STATE TITLES IN A ROW

On Friday, the Panthers walked through the school toward the coach bus that would take them to Utica and a state semifinal Class C ballgame against Lansing High School. Before boarding they were greeted by that familiar receiving line that was waiting for them with pats on the back and good luck wishes.

Once seated on the bus the boys waved goodbye. A succession of cars and the Ardsley police followed the bus to the New York State Thruway. Several cars even trailed the bus all the way to Utica.

On board the boys heard about Lansing, the Section 4 Far West Region champs, that made it to Utica on the strength of its pitching. Ardsley had its own pitching duo, Bernie McNerney and Steve Gyimesi. Lansing had senior Jack McDonald who was 12-0 for the season. Ardsley might have to face Matt Herrick who was 8-0 and struck out 16 in the Far West championship game. The Panthers wouldn't know who it would be until game time.

Friday afternoon the bus pulled into an Econo Lodge near Utica's ball field. Also staying there were many Ardsley fans. Coach Fitz wasn't happy the following morning because the team was up much of the night.

The usual format was for the semifinals and finals to be played on Saturday. Rain cut short that format and Ardsley only played one game that day. Coach Fitz meanwhile made plans for the team to move to the Sheraton Hotel if it made the finals.

Saturday morning the boys arrived at the Little Falls Veterans Memorial Park. Each youngster had his own thoughts when he got to the ball yard.

"When I got off the bus the only thing I was looking at was how far it was from home plate to the backstop," said catcher Tom Ferraguzzi. "It was ugly. It was far. Catching home games at Ardsley was so nice because the backstop was close. But I had some of my best defensive games at states because I was so worried that the balls would go to the backstop.

"I also remember getting off the bus and watching people who were looking at us and saying, 'That's Ardsley.' You always had to carry yourself in a certain way. I had to pretend that I was better or tougher than I really was. People actually knew us. They knew who we were. They knew we were coming after them.

"It was very windy and it was the first time I was on a real baseball field. Coach Fitz was talking and I couldn't even hear him because of the wind and the crowd screaming so much. During infield and outfield warm-ups I was nervous. I went out to catch Bernie and before the first pitch the glove was shaking in my hand. After that I was fine."

Tom Caldara had his own thoughts about these season ending games.

"Whenever you stepped off the bus and saw the minor league stadium it was one of the most magical feelings. You felt that this was such a privilege. It was such a treat. For kids who loved playing baseball it was like 'wow' how I'm able to walk out onto that beautiful grass and beautiful dirt. It felt so good.

"We always felt confident that we were expected to win. So when you get up and smell that grass and look at that field, you just feel that you are on top of the world. Let's get out there and start hustling. After a couple of years of winning, the confidence continues to grow so that you are more enticed by the magic of the stadium. Ardsley had also come to realize that reputations don't win ball games. Good performances win state titles.

Lansing, located on the Eastern shore of Cayuga Lake in the Finger Lakes district of New York, is best known as a small town close to Ithaca. In '89, it boasted about its high school Class C baseball team that finished the regular season 24-0 behind the strong pitching of Matt Herrick. That's who Ardsley would now face.

Herrick was undefeated, 8-0, had a 1.39 ERA, and averaged more than 14 strikeouts per game. In his previous two outings he struck out 34 batters.

Opposing Herrick was Ardsley's Bernie McNerney who knew it was an elimination game. He knew that in all likelihood it would be the last high school game he would ever pitch. He also knew about the game's magnitude.

In less than two innings the Panthers had figured Herrick out. Ardsley scored all the runs they needed in the second inning. Five runs crossed the plate as 11 players went to bat.

McNerney was staked to a 5-1 lead in the second inning before he served up a solo home run. He ran into trouble again in the sixth inning when he walked two and an error loaded the bases with one out. A two run single left Ardsley with a 6-4 advantage. Another walk loaded the bases again. That's when Ardsley's junior shortstop T.J. Rau saved the game. He ranged far to his right and caught a sinking line drive before it hit the ground.

As the game progressed all the innings Bernie had pitched began to take their toll. He began to tire. His shoulder started to ache in his attempt to keep the ball low. But he hung in there. By game's end Bernie had struck out 13 Lansing Bobcats and went out a winner. His varsity career ended with a 25-2 record.

Ardsley's 6-4 win meant the Panthers would play for a fourth consecutive state championship at Utica's Murnane Field, this time against Northern Adirondack, a rural community of about 8200 persons located in the foothills of the Adirondack Mountains, about 25 miles northwest of Plattsburgh and 25 miles west of Lake Champlain.

Sunday morning dawned sunny and beautiful. It was a day that belonged to Tom Caldara from beginning to end. On New York state's grandest high school baseball stage the junior second baseman not only led Ardsley at bat with a 3-for-4 performance, but also picked up the pitching save in Ardsley's 7-6 win.

The victory in front of 500 Ardsley fans gave the Panthers an unprecedented fourth consecutive state title and wrapped up a 26-2 season.

Capturing the states four years in a row was an incredible dream come true for the Ardsley boys. For Caldara it was a celebration of state titles won in each of his three varsity seasons. Following the 7-6 victory Tom was named the Tournament Most Valuable Player just as Bernie McNerney captured the same title a year earlier.

"Winning the states again means everything, not the MVP," Caldara told the *White Plains Reporter Dispatch* after the game. "The MVP award should have everybody's name on it."

The selection committee made the right decision in selecting Caldara. Whether it was driving in a winning run or pitching to close out a game, late inning heroics were customary for Tom throughout his career. Those heroics were expected by his fans and teammates.

Coach Fitz realized Caldara was an intense player dating back to his sophomore year. He knew he was always hard on himself and always concentrated on doing things correctly. He knew Tom's intensity was hard to duplicate and that it helped the team because it set an example for everyone else.

Gannett Westchester Newspapers named Caldara Player of the Year in 1989. In addition to the leadoff hitter's .510 batting average (51 for 100), he drove in 46 runs, and scored 40 runs. He also was Coach Fitz's go to relief specialist.

In the title game, besides his three hits, Caldara was effective in relief at the end just as Mike Ferraguzzi was in '88 and '89 when he also closed out state title wins. Caldara struck out four in the last two innings including the final three batters to end the game. Once that final out was recorded he was mobbed by Ardsley fans.

Caldara would later say that when there was one out in the last inning and all the Ardsley faithful moved from the bleachers down to the field he knew he would get the last two outs. He had come in for winning pitcher Steve Gyimesi with runners on first and third and no outs in the top of the sixth inning. He walked a batter to load the bases and then struck out the leadoff hitter on three pitches. The next batter doubled and Ardsley was holding on tightly to a 7-6 lead with Northern Adirondack runners on second and third.

Enter Ardsley third baseman Craig Stephens. The Northern Adirondack Bobcats No. 3 hitter lined a shot down the third baseline.

The ball was to Stephens right. Craig stretched his 6'5" frame caught the ball and doubled the runner off third base to end the rally. Craig later said that he knew Ardsley would win the game right then and there.

Years later, Caldara remembered entering the game in that sixth inning. "It was a little too close for comfort. I felt so confident in our team. It was one of those feelings that no one was going to stop us. With the momentum and confidence, it was never going to be in doubt that we were not going to win that game.

"I also remember being in the on deck circle. Dave Chenard batted ninth and I batted first and we were waiting to come up to the plate. We cracked jokes and laughed. Then we walked up to the plate. You would never have known how we were back in the on deck circle. We had the belief that no one was going to stop us. We had been through it so many times. It was high pressure but so much fun."

Ardsley put the game away by batting around and scoring three runs in the fourth inning. Caldara's triple off the left-center field wall scored T.J. Rau. That tied the game at 3-3. Jordan Polvere then hit into a fielder's choice that drove home Caldara and gave Ardsley the lead for good.

More Ardsley fielding plays helped cement the win. Northern Adirondack had runners at first and second in the fourth with one out. The Bobcats cleanup hitter drove a ball to right field. The wind kept carrying it towards the corner. T.J. Rau was playing right field. He caught the ball on the run and threw back to the infield so that the runners could not advance.

In the next inning, Caldara stretched a single to short center field into a RBI double. Steve Gyimesi, who went 3-for-4, singled to drive in Caldara. That gave the Panthers the winning run and the '89 Class C state title.

Soon the boys would be on the bus heading home. It was a bus ride they would remember the rest of their lives.

Tom Ferraguzzi recalls Coach Fitz coming on the bus after the win on Sunday and saying, "Wouldn't it be great guys if we could all show up and be on time for class tomorrow." 'Sorry Fitz' was the loud reply.

Hours later when the bus pulled up at the high school player relatives, friends, and children were there to greet the returning champions. One of the greeters was James Meinel's father Rusty who handed each of the players a cup of champagne when they left the bus.

The alcoholic partying continued into Sunday night at McDowell Park. That's when the Ardsley Police arrived. When told that the team had just won the state championship the police reply was 'Congratulations, just clean up.'

The next day it was time for the town of Ardsley to celebrate the win at the school's baseball field. Despite an early hour and sitting beneath a blazing sun, scores of people were there as the players sat on the bleachers and listened to speeches.

Coach Fitzpatrick told the crowd that Ardsley should treasure its 1989 title as if were the school's first. Joseph Gyimesi of the Panther Booster Association, whose son Steve starred on the team, said the team had all the qualities champions are made of...heart, spirit, talent, and hard work.

Then County Legislator Paul Feiner said there were not many things in life that are predictable: death, taxes and every year Ardsley winning the state baseball championship.

An Ardsley resident Ed Zimmer even donated $2,100 for a new batting cage.

The players had their own thoughts about what they had accomplished. Bernie McNerney said that winning the title four times was just like Joe DiMaggio's 56 game hitting streak. He said it would be a record that would never be broken. Since then no New York State school has won four titles in a row.

Steve Gyimesi recalled there were times when he was in the village and people would tell him that Ardsley couldn't win four in a row, that it was just impossible. Steve, who finished his career with a 16-0 record, said one of the reasons Ardsley did so well was because the team was prepared by playing in a tough league against teams like Eastchester, Westlake, Pelham and Peekskill.

"Coach Fitzpatrick gets us in the right frame of mind before a game and we usually don't make any mistakes," Gyimesi told *The*

White Plains Reporter Dispatch.

After the ceremony, the team left for a weekend at the Baseball Hall of Fame in Cooperstown, an outing they wanted instead of the usual parade.

There would be more baseball in Ardsley but now going on thirty years later there hasn't been another state title. In 1990 the Panthers had a great season going 25-2. Then in the state semifinal game at Veterans Stadium in Utica they played Rensselaer. There on June 9, 1990, the Ardsley dynasty came to a crashing halt. Rensselaer pounded three Ardsley pitchers for 15 runs in winning 15-1. Along with the end of Ardsley's streak of four consecutive state titles, the Panthers saw their string of 43 consecutive postseason victories come to a halt.

The Ardsley dynasty was now over. Years have passed since those four fabulous springs in the 1980s when a group of teenage Ardsley boys had a unique grip on the Village of Ardsley's psyche. Their youthful dreams became reality when they accomplished something that no other high school in the State of New York has duplicated. They were state champions for four straight years.

A.H.S. Baseball Champs 1989 — Bottom Row: (Left to Right) S. Gyimesi, B. McNerney. 2nd Row: J. Fanelli, J. Povere, T. J. Rau, T. Ferraguzzi, T. Caldara. 3rd Row: Coach N. Fitzpatrick, N. Reddy, C. Vicari, R. Brown, M. Morel, J. Tina. 4th Row: Coach Calaicone, M. Scallero, D. Chenard, C. Stevens, J. Meinel.

Bernie McNerney the ultimate competitor and unofficial leader of the team, the alpha dog.

Tom Caldara hits three-run homer in 17-1 win over Pine Plains.

Gannett Westchester Newspapers named Tom Caldara the Player of the Year in '89. He batted .510, drove in 46 runs, scored 40 times and was Coach Fitzpatrick's go to relief specialist.

Tom Caldara only Ardsley player to make four trips to play in state championship series.

Steve Gyimesi, three-time state champion, who Coach Fitzpatrick thought was the most draftable player he had ever coached.

Time to go to bat in '89.

Shortstop T.J. Rau, left, and Craig Stephens at third base during '89 title game.

Coach Fitzpatrick walks the line at '89 state championships.

Steve Gyimesi, Tom Caldara, Mike Morel and Bernie McNerney, left to right, enjoy the ride.

First Team All County, left to right, Bernie McNerney, Tom Caldara, and Steve Gyimesi.

Steve Gyimesi, Tom Caldara and Bernie McNerney, left to right, look to revise billboard by adding '89 title.

34. LIFETIME FRIENDSHIPS

The friendships contracted earliest in life, are those which stand by us the longest.

I wish I had been the first to utter those words. I wasn't. It was America's third president Thomas Jefferson. He knew what he was talking about.

If I had first read his words when I graduated from high school in Mount Vernon in 1960 I would have brushed them off and moved on with the conversation. But with each passing year, I've taken the words more to heart and can attest that they ring truer today than ever before.

And now that those 41 teenagers who played on those '86-'89 championship teams approach middle age, I'm quite sure they concur. Many still feel a sacred bond among themselves. They hold onto that bond. They are teammates for life.

These youngsters didn't play sports in Ardsley. They lived them. Baseball was the uplifting joy of their youth. They succeeded much more than they failed. In 1986 the team was 26-1; in 1987, 21-4; in 1988, 28-2, and 1989, 26-2.

Decades later, on athletic fields, golf courses or tennis courts they have done nothing that well since those high school playing days. That's when the game was best. That's when they got nervous and had butterflies, not the bad kind, the good kind. No athlete ever forgot those kind.

Tom Caldara's words speak volumes for many of his Ardsley baseball playing brethren when he talks about being at Bernie

McNerney's house. "We're in touch with Craig Stephens, Jordan Polvere, John Fanelli, James Minel, Mike Morel, Dave Chenard, and the Ferraguzzis," he said. "We're connected to each other.

"I just remember when I was in college the experience was great. But when I think about my high school friends, my baseball friends, it is with such love. Most of my friends through college had groups of friends. But it was so different. I felt I had more.

"At that age in high school you experience things so deeply. You are growing up. Your emotions are so raw. I think during that time when you experience all these things they stick with you so deeply. You are just a complete open innocent book. That's why we love thinking about Ardsley baseball when these things were happening.

"It was a gift. Every spring we had the gift of playing together at the highest level and winning the big ones regularly and being fortunate enough to carry the torch from the prior years. The best part too is how happy and how much pride the entire town had. They held these incredible celebrations.

"Every time you would stop somewhere in town during the baseball season, everyone connected with the community would be saying, 'Congratulations.' That made me feel good about how this little town was accomplishing something. It was community."

Today those boys hold on to those memories. They cherish them. It was a great time of their lives. For some, souvenirs and mementos like newspaper clippings and photographs are boxed away. Some even have videotapes of games played at the state championships.

For virtually all of Coach Fitz's boys who were part of those four championship teams it probably was their most incredible experience in sports. Things were just never the same after high school. College ball wasn't fun like it was in high school. It's quite different after high school. Coaches are more desperate.

"What's interesting to me having played college ball is that they make it more like a job," Caldara said. "You have guys on scholarships. You have coaches who need to keep their jobs and want to move in these tournaments and make money for their schools.

"In college it's still fun but it is ultimately big business and if you are playing at that high level you are also part of the pressure and desire to get closer to that next step of signing a professional contract. You can't replicate what you get back in Little League and then through high school, the beauty and innocence of playing the game for the love of the game.

"In the end, the perfect combination is doing the work, putting in the time, but also making it really fun. Fitz was able to do that. It all circles back to him. He gave us the chances and laid it out for us. There was the magic of that stage of being in high school and having all your friends."

Coach Neil Fitzpatrick impacted all their lives. Many became coaches because of him. Fitz loved coaching as a vocation not as a job. He always felt he was coaching future coaches and it was important for him to pass along the right values.

Even after being away from the game after all these years, he still deflects the credit due him. His constant refrain has been, "I had the horses to win, you have to have the horses to be successful."

In the late summer of 2016 when word got out that there was going to be the first-ever Ardsley Alumni Game on October 8 interest was high.

"Once former players found out that coach was going to be here and that he had been selected to the Westchester Sports Hall of Fame, it was just insane how quickly they wanted to say they would get here," said Jeff Caldara. The idea of an alumni game had bounced around in Jeff's head for several years. Caldara received an added boost when Coach Fitz agreed to attend.

Jeff had reached out to Paul Murphy who he hadn't spoken to in 20 years for help. Murphy was Caldara's mentor and along with Frank Constantino helped in getting Fitzpatrick inducted into the Hall of Fame.

By the time the festivities began there were over 108 former baseball players there who represented Ardsley classes from 1980 through 2016. A wonderful part of that day was the parents of players Fitzpatrick and Caldara had coached who showed up.

"At the festivities I didn't get a chance to introduce my wife Pam," Caldara said. "Pam introduced me. She said, 'To this day, my husband looks up to you Paul Murphy.'"

About 70 people found their way to the baseball diamond. Another 30 were on the sidelines mostly because their bodies had let them down over the years. More than 30 of the 70 on the diamond had their sons and daughters with them.

"Many took batting practice," Caldara said. "Fitz, like in the olden days, started throwing BP. He was dressed in old attire that he wore, shorts, high white socks, and a sweatshirt with 'Ardsley Baseball' emblazoned on it. It was no different. He was throwing strikes. The only difference was that he couldn't do it as long as he once could.

"The look on the guys faces was priceless. He predominantly threw to the guys he coached."

Fitzpatrick and Caldara are forever linked, both part of the continuum that is Ardsley baseball.

Take a look at the smiles on both their faces in the picture below. This was a moment frozen in time when the two of them were together at the Alumni Game.

Neil Fitzpatrick (left) and Jeff Caldara at 2016 at Ardsley Alumni Game.

Jeff smiles when he talks about the Alumni Game and his more than a chance meeting with Bob Grant. Grant's son RJ was a junior in 1998 and played on Caldara's first team as a head coach.

"One of the reasons we moved into the Ardsley district was because I was a baseball fan and the team had won the '86 state championship," Bob Grant told Caldara at the Alumni Game. Grant went on to tell Jeff how he, RJ, and daughter Kelly in '86, '87 and '88 would watch the team's championship parade pass by.

"For three years in a row, I stood there with my two little kids and watched you guys go by. It's fascinating now that one of those guys I walked by coached my son."

As a youngster, Jeff Caldara never saw it like that. Now by middle age, he realizes how cool it has been that the community is onboard with everything.

"That goes to show what this sport means to kids," Caldara said.

It's more than 48 years since Neil Fitzpatrick first stepped foot in Ardsley. If you wanted to find Neil today chances are you'll find him near his home on a tree-lined street, a short mile walk from the famous Saratoga Race Course in upstate New York.

He might be working on landscaping projects or out on the golf course polishing his game in hopes that someday he'll shoot his age. He might be sitting in his kitchen doing crossword puzzles. For the past 20 years he's entered the American Crossword Tournament. He also regularly works out at the local YMCA and even enters an occasional road race.

Once a month, when the mood strikes him, Neil will head south to Ardsley to visit his friends, Mike Kehoe and Hank Tina, both former Ardsley teachers.

At least once every spring Fitzpatrick will watch his one-time shortstop Jeff Caldara coach the Panthers in the shadows of Ardsley High School.

"I feel very good that Jeff Caldara is the coach," Fitzpatrick said. "He really instills great values in the next generation and I've witnessed the respect that his players have for him."

Watching Ardsley play, Neil in all likelihood takes a moment to stare at the back of the school at a beautiful running track that was once his high school baseball diamond. What he thinks about we'll never know. Soon he climbs into his car and heads home to Saratoga Springs with his memories.

Made in the USA
Middletown, DE
21 June 2018